Calves and Cubs

Beau Brannan

ISBN-13: 978-0-578-82174-0

SECTIONS

INTRODUCTION

I lost the game.

For those in the know, "the game" is to not think about the game...ugh I lost again.

Personal finance is also like a game, and like any game it requires having knowledge of the rules and principles in order to play it well. The difference with the personal finance "game" is that you automatically lose or forfeit if you *don't* think about it. For many, not thinking about the personal finance game is their default position. They not only don't know the rules, but they don't even know they are playing it!

If you have ever played camp games like "Bobby's World" or "this is a line," you know the frustration of being on the side of not knowing the rules of the game while everyone else does. The lack of understanding personal finance can be frustrating as well especially when there are others who seem to be in the know.

When we were we supposed to learn this?

We are certainly not lacking in information. We are not in short supply of "how-to invest" posts, courses, content, TikTok finance videos, r/wallstreetbets posts, mindset hacks and "get rich quick" strategies designed to help you gain riches and wealth fast. They make it seem so easy.

The disconnect for many is in understanding and applying that knowledge. For example, I can try to copy someone else's strategy in a game of chess, but if I don't understand the basics and do not know how to apply that strategy in different situations, the copied strategy quickly becomes a liability, especially when up against someone who knows the game. Put another way, the foundation of a house is built first, not the fun recreation room. If the foundation is built on solid ground, both it *and* the rec room can withstand all kinds of inclement seasons. A third example would be trying to jump into a book or TV series late. You might find some parts pleasurable, but you would never be able to fully experience it in its fullness.

The world of personal finance is vast and far reaching and the concepts are very much connected to each other. This book is designed for beginners and students with very little to no knowledge—especially those who are about to enter "real life" or "adulting" and haven't been fully educated in this space.

The objective of this book is not to give a "how-to" or "steps to financial freedom," but rather share a basic and foundational knowledge of personal finance terms and concepts with the goal of actually putting these into practice. There are certainly tremendous courses available online to go even deeper and the reader is encouraged to level up in whatever area is interesting or relevant.

There are certainly more nuances and rules and advanced concepts, but this book exists as an introduction. The content has been refined and derived from teaching personal finance courses to high school and college students. Not every finance topic is covered and arguably some basics are not included here. Take it for what it is—an introduction to get your bearings and begin to build a foundation. Ultimately you are responsible for your own education and decision making. When you take ownership of things, reality changes for you.

I have chosen to refer to this subject as Personal Finance as opposed to Financial Literacy for no other reason than to remind ourselves, we must take *personal* responsibility for our finances.

The content is specific to the United States, but most principles are universal. This book does not give specific financial or investment advice. As always, consult a professional (or if it applies to you, your parents) before making any financial decisions. The information is being presented without consideration of the investment objectives, risk tolerance or financial circumstances of any specific investor and might not be suitable for all investors. Oh, and one more thing: **past performance of the market or what other investors have done in the past or say they've done on TikTok does not guarantee future results or success.**

TIME

YOUNG AND [*ADJECTIVE*]

[Monologue]: "I read this article a while back that said that Microsoft employs more millionaire secretaries than any other company in the world. They took stock options over Christmas bonuses. It was a good move. I remember there was this photograph of one of the groundskeepers next to his Ferrari. Blew my mind. You see s*** like that, and it just plants seeds. Makes you think it's possible—even easy. And then you turn on the TV, and there's just more of it. The $87 million lottery winner. That kid actor that made $20 million on his last movie. The internet stock that shot through the roof. You could have made millions on it if you just got in early. And that's exactly what I wanted to do. Get in. I didn't want to be an innovator, I just wanted to make a quick and easy buck. I just wanted in[1]…"

Whether or not you relate to this, certainly you understand the desire. Before you listen to people sharing or selling you on how you can be rich or wealthy; it is important you understand and define for yourself what these terms even mean. In addition to defining your terms, it is also critical to know yourself and your tendencies. No sense studying investing if you tend to overspend and often go into debt.

---

[1] Monologue by the character Seth Davis in Boiler Room (film), 2000.

Take a moment to grab a pen and paper or use the back of this book. Physical pen and paper are the best, but typing is ok too. Something different occurs when you physically write as opposed to just thinking, so please indulge the request for your benefit.

When you hear the words "rich" and "wealthy" ...

- What images come to mind? *Write them out on that paper.*
- What are you doing? *Write it out on that paper.*
- What are you feeling? *Write it out on that paper.*
- Where are you? Are you in a different location than now? *Describe it on that paper.*

Now, as you read and reflect on your responses, consider this:

You can be rich, but not wealthy.

You can also be wealthy, but not rich.

But you could be both.

Think about and define what being **rich** is, and what having **wealth** truly means. Write this down as well. In your personal definitions consider there are things in this life that are priceless and money could never buy. Ask yourself what those priceless things might be for you personally and write them down as well.

IS IT POSSESSION OF TIME OR TIME OF POSSESSION?

If you are young, you are most likely in a position where you personally do not have a lot of money to your name. But there is something you possess (or possesses you) even *more* valuable—**Time**.

We often forget about time because we cannot see it. Sure, we mark it and repeatedly glance at clocks, watches and calendars. Sometimes we feel it when a class moves slow, or a vacation goes too fast, but it doesn't feel the same as money leaving your hands.

Time is quite scarce, it cannot be hoarded, it cannot be mined, it is an equalizer. Daily, we get 1440 minutes regardless of who we are and how diverse our backgrounds could be.

But our time is constantly being spent and traded for some-*thing*. We trade or exchange our time to be entertained, to rest, create, learn, numb ourselves, socialize, etc.

Time does not stop and is always working on everyone, everywhere no matter where we are geographically. And while we get to make choices about where and how to spend our time, it can also be working *for us* and/or *against us* in other areas of our life at the same moment.

In other words, time can also be understood as an **asset.** An asset is something (like an investment) which generates income, money or value passively. Passively means with little-to-no extra effort on your part, or "while you sleep." The mindset of those who are "well-off financially" (whatever that means to you) is that they tend to be **asset minded**. This means instead of looking for things to spend money on, consume, or flex, they are looking for assets—things which will earn money or create wealth or grow in value.

Time therefore, works for them. In their favor, not against them.

Here is an extreme but true example. The year is 2001 and your jam is "Get Ur Freak On" by Missy Elliott. Apple advertises the new iPod where you can have "1,000 songs in your pocket" by carrying a portable device holding your MP3 song files and weighing a little more than a billiard ball—all for $399. You buy it and feel great about this luxury. Your headphones are in, the world is tuned out and your pod is loaded with Nickelback and Creed albums that you paid $9.99 for.

But let's say you decided instead to spend that same $399 purchasing an asset, like stock in Apple instead of buying an iPod. If you did, then today you would have approximately $285,850! To be clear, not all stocks do this. This is a freak example but is used to demonstrate how time and money do a sort of collaboration. This would be considered as being "asset minded." Whereas the spender in this case, has a 2001 iPod which is likely gone or broken.

A good first self-awareness question to ask yourself is: are you more of a spender, a saver, or an investor?

If you aren't sure, just look and follow the money. You can say you are an investor, but if all your money is spent on in-game purchases on Fortnite or Clash of Clans, then you are a spender. There is no judgment on what you are, but you need to know in order to make changes/maintain your discipline.

Take a moment and remember that we spend and use our time to gain material things like money, possessions and space. How do you personally view time? How do you treat it? Are you aware of how you currently use and spend it?

THE COMPOUND EFFECT

There is a popular personal finance question about whether you would rather choose between two options:

1. $3 Million cash right now

2. OR a Penny which will double for 30 days

Usually when you ask this question people assume there is a trick or a game, so they instinctively choose the penny that doubles, but don't know why they pick the penny.

The penny that doubles everyday chart looks like this:

DAY 1 $.01	**DAY 11** $10.24	**DAY 21** $10,485.76
DAY 2 $.02	**DAY 12** $20.48	**DAY 22** $20,971.52
DAY 3 $.04	**DAY 13** $40.96	**DAY 23** $41,943.04
DAY 4 $.08	**DAY 14** $81.92	**DAY 24** $83,886.08
DAY 5 $.16	**DAY 15** $163.84	**DAY 25** $167,772.16
DAY 6 $.32	**DAY 16** $327.68	**DAY 26** $335,544.32
DAY 7 $.64	**DAY 17** $655.36	**DAY 27** $671,088.64
DAY 8 $1.28	**DAY 18** $1310.72	**DAY 28** $1,342,177.28
DAY 9 $2.56	**DAY 19** $2621.44	**DAY 29** $2,684,354.56
DAY 10 $5.12	**DAY 20** $5242.88	**DAY 30** $5,368,709.12

Based on the chart, it appears the doubling penny choice is the move. Over $5 Million certainly beats $3 Million!

Even if you thought you could double your $3 Million with your own efforts in just one month, that would be a difficult task and certainly requires more risk and effort than simply waiting 30 days. All things being equal, the penny appears to be the right choice.

But there is a catch. The only way the penny is the best choice is if you start day one and let it go for the full 30 days. If you decided to wait before starting the doubling process, even delaying just one day, then the $3 Million cash up front was by far the better offer.

The chart is mesmerizing to see how a penny, which for many of us is not even worth picking up on the street, doubling for 30 days can lead to over 5 Million Dollars. The explanation of the phenomenon is that the penny is experiencing the **compound effect.** In this case it means interest (typically understood as the cost of borrowing money) is compounded, or grows exponentially. To put another way, the penny is earning interest on top of the interest already earned. And the process keeps going and going and going.

Now obviously pennies don't magically double on their own, but if the cost for someone to borrow that penny from you was actually 100% interest per day, then the chart is how it would play out for the next 30 days.

To explain further. Let's say you want to see a movie at the theatre ($10 student rate), but you are out of money. Me being the great friend that I am, lend you or let you borrow my $10 for one week and we agree that you will pay me back $11 when we hang out again next Saturday. I am effectively charging you 10%

interest (a dollar in this case) to borrow my money for one week.

To make it more serious, we also agree that I will charge you 10% interest *compounded* every week until you pay me back. (Of course, if we're good friends and I don't charge interest then you give me $10 at the end of the week and everything is cool. It is worth noting here that a great way to destroy friendships is to charge interest on small sums of money).

But let's say I am serious about the interest, and you don't pay me back for a second week. So, I charge you *another* 10% on top of the $11 you owe me, which is $1.10! This makes your new payment now $12.10 ($11 + $1.10). Here is how it looks for the next month if you don't pay.

Week 1 - $11 ($10 x 10%)

Week 2 - $12.10 ($11 x 10%)

Week 3 - $13.21 ($12.10 x 10%)

Week 4 - $14.31 ($13.21 x 10%)

That borrowing of $10 is starting to get expensive.

MENTAL MATH

move the decimal over left for 10%

75.00 → 7.500 OR 7.50

10% of 75.00 is 7.50

want to leave a 20% tip?

If bill is $25.00

25.00 X 2 = $5

Back to the penny. In the very unrealistic scenario of the doubling penny, you are getting a 100% interest rate compounded daily. Again, not realistic in the real world but here is the whole point of the "doubling" penny example:

> **If you wait or delay even just a day, you miss out on a lot of potential upside and future growth. Get going today!**

Remember, time is an asset!

Like our example of borrowing the $10 for 10% interest per week, you can be on the other side of this compound effect. If you keep neglecting or forgetting to pay me, the amount keeps growing. If you waited a whole year that means the amount you owe compounds 52 times! because our terms were that I would charge you 10% every week compounded you didn't return the money. Your $10 that you owe me at the end of one year is $1420! Great for me, but terrible for you.

Week 3 - $13.21
Week 4 - $14.31
....
Week 52 - $1420

Compounding is amazing when it works for you and devastating when it works against you. One other variable to keep in mind with compound interest is *when* or *how often* the amount is compounded.

LAW OF 72

when an investment will double

72 ÷ interest rate

ex: 3% annual interest

72 ÷ **3** = 24 Years for investment to double

Most often, interest is based on a one-year timeframe, sometimes called APY or (annual percentage yield). If you have $1000 in an account that pays interest, at the end of the year (with 1% interest or 1% APY) you get $10. It is important to look at how often interest is calculated. Again, typically it is based annually or every year.

Go back and look at the penny chart one more time. In your mind, change the days to years. If you choose to wait to start with this unrealistic doubling penny example until Year 5 (or when you graduate college), you won't get over $5 Million anymore, you will only get approximately $167,000. Crazy the difference that 5 years can make! Again, there is a time value of money.

So why haven't you started yet?

People wait or delay for all sorts of reasons. Some reasons are understandable, but many are just excuses. If you get anything out of this book it would be to find a way to start **TODAY**. Find a way to start putting your money to work. Even if you created a system or a rule for yourself to save 5 cents a day, momentum starts to occur. You are more likely to save beyond 5 cents a day because you have started a habit.

Do not say, "I don't have any money to save" because you can always find a way to acquire a penny or a nickel every day. There are even apps like Acorns which will round up your purchases you make with your debit card and invest the change. If your meal was $8.75, Acorns rounds up and takes $0.25 and invests it. This shouldn't be your sole investing, but the point is there really is no excuse to start.

But this concept of starting today and compounding isn't just relevant in terms of money. The compound effect occurs in our lives and the decisions we make.

In our own lives the choices we make may seem very small like a penny, but they do compound.

Think about this: no one chooses to be a drug addict or morbidly obese. Yes, there may have been events and circumstances, maybe even genetics that were out of that person's control, but by and large it was a small decision repeated over and over. It compounded and became for many people, insurmountable and/or very difficult to get out of. Again, I do not take lightly or ignore mental health issues or genetic predispositions that may be tied into some of these decisions. The fact remains that our choices no matter how insignificant or small they seem, do matter.

The next step is to think about what you want, and who you want to be, so you can start making those positive small decisions every day, which compound. But it is difficult to move toward those goals and visions if you don't know where you currently stand.

YOUR GOALS & DREAMS

Let's assume we are at a weird futuristic carnival and one of the games you can play requires throwing a dart at a target or a dartboard. Here is where it gets a little weird. The closer to the bullseye (or center) you land the dart, the better your life will be from that point forward. You also get a choice between a dartboard which moves around erratically or a dartboard that is stationary and attached to a wall. With your future happiness at stake, which would you pick?

While the moving target might be a fun challenge it wouldn't be if your happiness depends on it. You would go with the stationary/fixed target option.

This may seem like a ridiculous analogy, but many people in life unknowingly select the moving target. They select the moving target because they never take the time to consider their goals, desires, systems and plans. They don't pay attention to their habits or know their context. These same people wonder why it is so hard to live the life they want. They blame culture, the government, or just straight up complain about everything. Oftentimes it is because they are metaphorically trying to throw a dart at an erratically moving dartboard. In some cases, they aren't even aware the goal is to hit the dartboard at all!

At this point, please complete Appendix A and Appendix B at the back of the book. You will notice the very first activity is to anchor yourself in gratitude and appreciation and thankfulness for the things you do have. Before you begin to think about things you want to do, have and be, write out the most significant things you are grateful for. This helps offset an unhealthy and envious approach to life and many times refocuses us. It also helps to curb complaining. Therefore, not just on this but in life **gratitude should be a daily practice and discipline**.

BUDGETING & SAVING

All SYSTEMS GO

Now that you have established your goals, and are aware of your habits and current context, the next step is to learn how discipline leads to freedom and the life you are building.

The word discipline for many evokes images of punishment, groundings, timeouts, etc. In sports, it may evoke images of extra sprints. But it is better to think of discipline in terms of its original concept and usage—training and instruction.

We all know the importance of eating healthy, exercising, and sleep. We also know there is a level of discipline required in these areas. If you want to eat healthier, you must be disciplined about what you eat. This may mean if a meal comes with french fries, you "train" or "instruct" or discipline yourself to choose non-fried vegetables or a salad instead.

If you are aiming to be more agile or athletic or simply more fit, then it requires discipline to work out consistently.

Money is no different. Just as you cannot expect an obese person to lose weight by wishing it off, you cannot expect someone to stay out of money troubles without a budget. And you cannot expect to be rich and/or wealthy (however you define those) or maintain it without a plan (budget) and discipline.

There are many ways to create a budget. There are plenty of apps to easily help you start and maintain one. There are spreadsheet templates and other methods. No matter what you use, the key is to actually use it and be consistent. The basis of every budget is to assign every single dollar a place to go and a job to do.

Remember, a budget does not mean punishment, killjoy, or boring. It isn't about what you can't have, but more about efficiently helping you get to what you actually want. A budget is more like weights in a gym. You cannot get stronger if you don't lift heavy things and you cannot grow your finances without a budget.

The problem for many is the habit of spending and perhaps even saving without a purpose or goal. For instance, instead of budgeting for new shoes, Kevin just looks to see if he has the money in his account (or just hopes there is) and buys the shoes because he wants to. Kevin then complains about how he never has enough money to hang out with friends and is always stressed out about money.

If Kevin had used a budgeting system, then he would be more likely to get his shoes, hang out with friends, *and* build for his future.

But let's say Kevin is blessed and hasn't had to worry about money because his parents just give it to him. Even then, without building discipline he is setting himself up for future loss. There are stats suggesting 70% of wealthy families lose their wealth in the second generation and 90% by the third[2].

With the importance of discipline and budgets in mind, a helpful visual image for a budget is to imagine envelopes each marked

---

[2]https://www.marketwatch.com/story/heres-why-90-of-rich-people-squander-their-fortunes-2017-04-23

with a specific category.

Here is a sample for a younger student named Sam with an allowance of $525 a month.

The amount and type of envelopes depends on your needs. But note there is an envelope labeled, "gifts" anticipating those annual and infrequent purchases like holiday shopping or maybe your significant other's birthday.

The idea here is that you are planning a year in advance instead of living day to day, or impulsively. A couple other envelopes to create are to pay yourself (listed above as "savings") and charity. The charity envelope is optional but giving habitually actually benefits you mentally and financially because it creates more discipline. Not to mention it makes the world a better place for others. At the end of the day, your legacy is in how you treat others, not in how much money you have.

The above constitutes Sam's budget for the month, and she can always adjust. If she overspends in one category, then she can take it from another and readjust. The goal is to be balanced and not overspend.

The other aspect Sam wants to aim for is to make sure this money is from last month. In other words, if Sam gets paid $2000 on May 1, she wants this $2000 to be her budgeting money for the month of June. Ideally Sam is using April's money for the living expenses in May. This is less stressful than getting paid on May 1 and living on that money in the month of May. This is also called living "paycheck to paycheck" and may be necessary for a season but is not healthy.

Again, you do not need to use (and probably shouldn't) physical envelopes stuffed with cash, but the mental model is helpful in knowing where and how to put each dollar to work. Again, there are apps which can do all of this for you. What a time to be alive. Find a system right now, set up your budget and run with it!

Another incentive to consider is to offer yourself a bonus. For example, many businesses will offer bonuses if budgets come in underspent. Meaning if there is a **surplus** (money not spent from the category) in the company budget, then the unspent money is given back to employees as a bonus and "thank you" for being responsible.

Feel free to do the same for yourself. The wise and long-term bonus would be to take that money and invest it or put it toward acquiring an asset, but life is also a gift and meant to be enjoyed so maybe you want to reward yourself by putting it toward a travel experience in the near future.

The point here is to make a budget something you view as helpful, necessary and dare I say...fun. Make it a game, whatever you got to do.

As you begin to budget, if you are feeling constrained or aren't sure how to fit everything in, there may be ways to "find" money based on how you currently spend.

For example, you may have a habit of getting an iced coffee from your favorite coffee joint every morning. Let's say your coffee costs $3.00. If you get this every day you are spending over $1,000 a year on iced coffee! In the moment, $3 doesn't seem like much but the repeated transaction sure adds up.

If you decide to make iced coffee at home even 2-3 days a week, you begin to "free" up some money. Or perhaps your office has coffee provided and you decide to use that instead. Sure, it may be a sacrifice, but it is worth it if you are freeing up a substantial amount of money. Imagine if that money is not just saved but it starts to work for you! "Penny pinching" is a great discipline, but again income streams and assets are what you really want to focus on. Allow both mindsets to work for you. Work smarter, not harder.

Because of how critical and foundational a budget is, **only if you have constructed your budget may you continue onto the next topic.**

SAVINGS/SAVINGS ACCOUNTS

After having set up your budget and giving every single dollar a place to go and a job to do, you need a place to store and build up savings. This is important for emergencies because life happens. You may have heard the expression "saving for a rainy day." There will be days which are not ideal, and it is nice to know you have a fund from which you can draw when these times arise.

The recommendation is to have 3-6 months of living expenses in **savings**. When you are young, this is more about the discipline of saving money but can also be used for special and fun events as they come up.

Many students are fortunate to have their parents cover expenses and special events like Prom, or Fraternity dues, but for many students that is their responsibility. So, where to put this money?

You could keep it in your drawer or in your mattress at home, but if your home is robbed or destroyed in a fire, no one replaces that money. Another reason to consider is that the world is becoming more and more dependent on electronic payments. For instance, on an airline you cannot purchase meals or drinks with cash anymore, you must use a card or electronic payment which relies on having an account for this purpose. COVID-19 has also accelerated more electronic payments.

A common place to deposit your money and set up an account is with a **bank**. The bank keeps your money safe and does the basic accounting for you. You know exactly how much you have as well as a record of when and where you spend.

A bank also insures your money so that if the bank ceases to exist, your money is insured by **FDIC** (Federal Deposit Insurance Corporation) up to $100,000. This means if the bank where you keep your money went bankrupt tomorrow, you would be able to recover the money paid out by FDIC insurance. You get access to this insurance by depositing money with the bank.

You may be thinking: "Wait, why would a bank go bankrupt? They are banks!"

Yes, banks are typically very safe. But it is important to remember that banks are businesses.

Here is how banks work on a <u>very basic</u> level and how they make their money.

To start, let's dispel a myth. For some there is an image that if I deposit my money at the bank, the bank teller takes my money and secures it in a vault for me. While it is true there are *safety deposit boxes* where you can keep some possessions and cash safe, this is not the main purpose of a bank.

Instead, the bank takes your money and then credits you the amount you deposited. Let's say you deposited $100. You then open up your fancy banking app and you see in your account +$100. Then what the bank will do in theory is take that money and then go make money off *your* money. Banks make money by loaning money out for cars, homes, small businesses, etc. for a certain interest rate. Recall the earlier conversation on interest.

The bank takes that $100 and pools it with other people's deposited money and loans it out to an individual. Banks also deposit and borrow money from the **Federal Reserve** (think of it as a bank for banks) so they aren't solely dependent on how many people deposit money. A discussion on Federal Banking, the Reserve or monetary policy is beyond the scope of this introduction. But to give an example of loans, let's say an individual is looking to buy a car.

The bank loans out $25,000 for the individual to buy a car at an interest rate of 5% for 60 months (5 years).

If the individual makes regular monthly payments then in five years, the bank will make about $3300 on that loan. Now imagine doing these deals and even bigger deals multiple times. Banks can make some good money.

To incentivize or encourage you to "keep your money safe" with them, they offer you some interest as well because technically, they are borrowing *your* money. The rate they give you is significantly less, because they are a business and trying to make money too. They have salaries and buildings and expenses to pay.

If you look at most banks, currently they will offer significantly less than 1% interest. This is not a good rate for making money. But banks set this number based on the **Federal Interest rate** (the rate it costs the bank to borrow from the Federal Reserve) so if the rate is low there, it will be low at the bank. Consult your local Economics teacher or professor to explore further the topic of Prime and Federal Interest Rates.

On the topic of "not a good rate for making money," there is another "I" beyond **interest** to be aware of when thinking about your money, **inflation**.

This also is a "force" potentially working against you. Perhaps you have heard your grandparents or even parents make a comment like, "back in my day, we could buy gas for 49 cents a gallon." Or "back in my day, a soda cost 25 cents in the vending machine."

Of course, with an eye roll your initial thought is "OK Boomer." But here is the sad reality...you will do the same thing. You will tell your kids how you could have a full meal at Taco Bell for $5 when they are now paying $10! May it never be so!

What happened? Inflation. This simply means the value of money loses its purchasing power over time. It is almost like it decays.

If I gave you a $5 bill today and you put it inside a book and then 20 years later you find it again, you will not be able to buy as much as you did today. Now there are other economic forces involved in inflation and at what rate this money inflates, but for our purposes just know that putting money in a savings account and earning even a generous 1% interest (if you are lucky) does not mean you are making money. Because there is another force at play working against you called inflation. You can always search the current inflation rate at any time.

With bank basics in mind, there is another option on where to keep your money and that is at a **Credit Union**. Credit Unions have the same services as a bank. The difference is a Credit Union is owned by its members (essentially those who bank there) and is not a traditional business. Credit Unions still make money off your money, but Credit Unions can often offer better rates than a traditional bank because they do not have the same expenses and do not answer to shareholders (those who own stock in the banks). There are pros and cons to a traditional bank vs a credit union so you would just need to decide what your needs are.

Finally, there are **online bank** options. Online banks also offer competitive interest rates because they typically do not have physical branches or banks to sustain. But that can be the downside as well, since many online banks do not have "brick and mortar" locations or physical banks you may be unable to access certain services. If you do not need anything beyond a place for money to come in and an occasional bill to pay, this could be a very viable option. Again, do your research.

On that note of an account with money coming in and going out, let's look at a specific type of "bank account" set up for this purpose. The first account we have been alluding to is a **savings account**, which is intended to save a certain amount of money for emergencies or special reasons and earn you some interest (but as we saw, don't rely on it). There are limits on how often you may withdraw or take-out money in a savings account. If you set up a savings account, look for the rules, fees and interest rates. These accounts often require minimum deposit amounts or will charge fees if you don't deposit enough money.

Finally, it is worth considering if you do have a substantial amount of money in a savings account, ask whether that is working for you or against you. Perhaps a portion of that money could be invested or maybe moved to a different type of account. Many people, when young were instructed to place birthday money and graduation money into a savings account. As they get older, they forget to revisit this money and oftentimes miss out on opportunities to grow and compound that money.

For more flexibility with moving money let's look at checking accounts.

CHECKING/CHECKING ACCOUNTS

A **checking account** is the type of bank account you write checks out of. While writing checks are becoming more obsolete, the concept of money going in (**deposit**) and money going out (**withdrawals**) remains the same. The most common way to pay from this account is by using a **debit card**. When you pay for a meal or item, the money is deducted from your checking (or debit) account. The other option is to withdraw cash from an ATM (automatic teller machine). At the machine you insert your debit card, type in your pin number and you may withdraw cash from your checking or savings account. Pin numbers are assigned when you receive your card in the mail, but you may also set them at a physical bank and sometimes over the phone.

A checking account does not typically pay you interest to deposit money there because the money is moving in and out regularly.

But this is the account you would use to pay bills or make regular purchases. This is also the account you may want to set up a **direct deposit**. This is sometimes designated as an **ACH** payment (ACH means Automated Clearing House). It is simply an electronic transfer or payment between accounts. If you work and your employer offers the service (most do), you can have your paycheck sent directly to your checking account. You do not need to take a paper check to the bank or scan on your phone with your banking app, the money transfers automatically.

It is worth mentioning that while checks are not as prevalent, blank checks with your information are offered to you for a nominal fee (to pay for printing and shipping) when you open a checking account. The graphic below is a quick primer of how a check works and how to write a check.

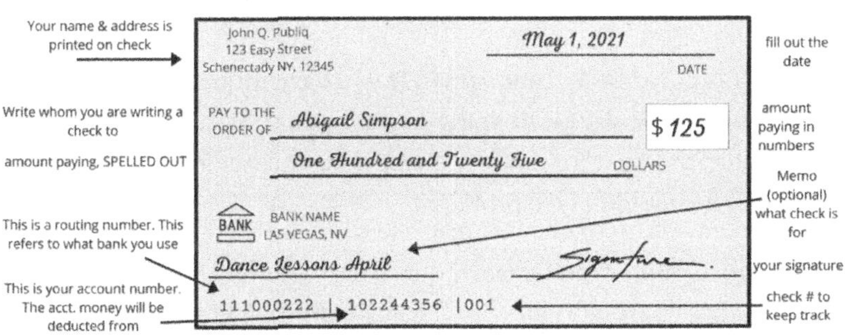

As you set up either a checking or savings account, be sure to fully understand the fees, penalties and rules. Again, many times banks require a minimum amount of money to be deposited or else they charge a fee. Banks may also charge a fee if you **overdraft**. An overdraft means you took out more money than you actually have in the account. You may link or connect your savings and checking accounts together and sign up for **overdraft protection**. This allows the overdraft to occur without a penalty because it will take the extra money from another account. Each bank is slightly different, so just make sure you know all the fees and penalties up front and do what you can to avoid them.

CD'S/MONEY MARKET ACCOUNTS

If you are considering keeping your money safe in a savings account but would like to get a little bit more interest, there are a couple other options to consider.

One option would be to open a **CD**. CD's in the finance world stand for **certificate of deposit**. If you are willing to "lock up" your money away for a specific period of time, the bank or credit union will offer you a little more interest on your money. With a CD you are effectively telling the bank, "I promise I will not touch this money for a specified period of time." For doing so, they pay out a tad more interest than a savings account.

This could be a viable option if you have money you are saving for a particular event in the future but don't want the temptation of spending it (of course since you have a budget that you stick to, it shouldn't be a problem).

Since money can be taken out of savings and checking accounts rather easily (also known as being **liquid**), CD's require more work to take money out. While you may take money out early, you do forfeit the money you would have made from interest. In some cases, there may even be more penalties. It is always best to leave it in the CD if you can.

To give an example, let's say you have enough money saved up for a Europe trip next summer. You could place your money into a CD for a one year period. It is safe and when you "open it" after 1 year, you get a little more interest than if you had put it in a savings account. At current rates it may pay for an extra espresso or two on your trip, but it is better than nothing. Search current CD rates online to see the latest offerings.

CD Ladder

An advanced player move with CD's is to set up something called a **CD ladder**. There are different ways to structure them, but here is one way to do it so you get the idea.

Let's say you have $500 saved. You go to the bank or credit union and at the same time you purchase five different CD's with $100 in each. I have included an interest rate (although these are not accurate at current rates). Here is what you bought:

A 5 year CD (at 1.50%), a 4 year CD (at 1.25%), a 3 year CD (at 1.00%), a 2 year CD (at .75%) and a 1 year CD (at .50%)

When the 1-year CD matures or the year is up, you "open" the CD and take that money (the $100 you put in plus the interest you made, which would be 50 cents). Then you purchase a new 5-year CD, putting $100.50 into that new 5-year CD.

In year 2, the 2-year CD is opened and you take that money ($100 plus the interest earned over the last 2 years, or $1.50) and purchase another new 5-year CD, putting in $101.50

In year 3, you open the 3-year CD and buy a 5-year CD and the process keeps repeating.

The idea is that you are safely growing your money over a period of time. You can keep this ladder going as a cascade, or if you want to run it once you can get a better return on 5 years of your money than placing it in a savings account for 5 years. Again, this is purely a savings strategy and not an investment strategy.

Money Market Accounts

A money market account is another savings option. You may see them also described as **money market deposit account** (MMDA), or just **money market account** (MMA). These accounts will typically offer a little more interest than a savings account as well, but also require a bigger deposit amount. They tend to have the same restrictions on how many checks or withdrawals you can make per month. This account isn't for daily use, but is a slightly better savings account option to consider if you have larger periodic expenses such as tuition payments, or property taxes.

In both cases of the CD and the MMA, you are giving up either more **time** or more **money** in exchange for more interest.

You can see how the *time value of money* plays out in these savings options.

Finally, it is worth noting that the interest you make in any of these savings accounts are taxable. It is considered a type of income.

Oof, so it begins...

TAXES

Taxes are one of those topics people wonder why they weren't taught in school. Perhaps you have seen memes and posts lamenting how school teaches things like the hypotenuse of a triangle and vertical asymptotes, but not taxes—something which impacts us every day. Even if taxes are taught in school, taxes are hard to focus on and be interested in when you aren't dealing with them at the moment.

You already know—death and taxes are certainties in life. Indeed, there are all sorts of taxes we encounter in our life. Since taxes are complex, it is important to know that there are different rules in different states and different countries. The purpose here is to hit on the tax basics common to most, if not all of us. This is not a definitive guide to taxes, "but only a tribute[3]." As a reminder, this section is specific to living in the United States.

Some of the more common taxes you encounter in life are **income tax, FICA** tax (Social Security and Medicare), and **sales tax.** Other taxes you might experience such as property taxes and capital gains taxes will be explored a little later.

The first two, income tax and FICA relate to taxing money you earn as income.

Sales tax refers to taxing money related to how much you spend.

To put crudely, what you eat is taxed and most of what comes out on the other end is taxed as well.

---

[3] And this is a tribute to "Tribute" by Tenacious D

Sales Tax

We will start with sales tax first. Although some states do not have sales tax (Alaska, Delaware, Montana, New Hampshire, and Oregon) all other states do and they range in the amount or percentage they charge.

As a basic example, if you go to Big Rick's Clothing Barn to buy a hooded sweatshirt and the price tag says $20.00 you will also pay sales tax (assuming you aren't in the states listed above). This can be a combination of state, county and city. Again, it can vary from place to place, even within the same state. But in general, you will pay sales tax on the sweatshirt amount. If the sales tax rate is 5% then you will pay $1.00 (5% of $20 = $1.00) or $21.00 total. The business then remits the tax to the required agencies.

Generally, food and food products sold by food stores are exempt from sales tax but a couple states do charge sales tax on food. This does not include prepared food. Buying an apple for 50 cents at the grocery store would be 50 cents when you check out, but buying chicken tenders at a drive-thru or even at the grocery store is taxable. There are other items ranging from cigarettes to alcohol to soda to gasoline that can carry even more sales tax. These vary from state to state and county to county.

With that in mind here is a quick tangent. In our example above the sweatshirt cost over $20. But think about what you needed to do to earn that $20.

If you work part-time and you get paid a very generous $20/hour, then on paper you would think you just needed to work one hour to buy that sweatshirt. Not so fast. That $20 not only has sales tax on the backend (an extra 5% in our example) but you also get taxed on the front end on your income before you even get the money to spend.

That $20 sweatshirt therefore requires *more* than an hour of work to pay for it. Remembering this can help to curb frivolous spending when you realize you are always paying more than what the price tag or menu says. It is certainly worth converting a bigger purchase into time to give you a different perspective. In other words, try to calculate how long you need to work in order to earn the purchase.

Income Tax

Without commentary or getting political, the concept of income tax (as well as sales tax) is intended to fund the government and the services meant to help the general public and those in most need. How well the government uses this money is up to you to decide.

The amount of income tax you pay is based on how much you make in income. This could be from a job or some other income stream like investments. The income is taxed by the Federal government, but there are also states which charge income tax as well. Most do.

The states that do not charge state income tax are: Alaska, Florida, New Hampshire, Nevada, South Dakota, Tennessee, Texas, Washington, and Wyoming.

We'll start with Federal first. Federal income tax is considered a **progressive tax**. Progressive simply means the more you make, the more you pay. There is also what is called a **regressive tax** which goes the other direction—the less you make, the more you pay. Sales tax is an example of regressive tax because it does not care if you are rich or poor. A millionaire pays the same for chicken tenders in sales tax as does someone with only $100 to their name. This tax obviously has a bigger impact proportionally on the low-income person; hence it is regressive.

The progressive income tax brackets which show how much you pay in Federal income taxes typically have minor changes every year, and are publicly available to view. The thing to remember is <u>not every dollar gets taxed the same.</u>

Here is an abbreviated Federal tax bracket chart for an individual taxpayer. It does not include every bracket so feel free to look up the most current and complete chart.

TAX RATE	TAXABLE INCOME RANGE	TAX OWED
10%	$0 to $9,875	10% of taxable income
12%	$9,876 to $40,125	$987.50 plus 12% of the amount over $9,875
22%	$40,126 to $85,525	$4,617.50 plus 22% of the amount over $40,125

If the chart is confusing, don't worry. Let's learn how to read it. We will consider the case of Madison, who is 22 years old with her first job working at Applebee's and not married.

Above is what the federal income chart looks like for her as an **individual filer.** (If you are married and have a **joint filing status**, then the chart has different amounts because you are combining your money with a spouse or partner, hence "joint").

FYI, there are really great calculators online which get a more exact figure, but the explanation below is to give a general sense for how it works.

Madison makes $55,000 a year at Applebee's (wow!). This is her **gross income**. This is how much she makes before any taxes or expenses.

Before we start the tax calculation, Madison is entitled to a **standard deduction** on her taxes. More on this later, but just know the government anticipates there are basic and essential expenses you need to live and work and the government gives a reprieve or allows you to **deduct** from your taxable amount.

The standard deduction amount is $12,400 (as of publishing). There may be other expenses you have which exceed $12,400 and you can choose to itemize those instead. But right now, we will assume the standard deduction.

Therefore, to get an accurate picture of Madison's taxes we will deduct $12,400 from her gross income of $55,000. Her more accurate taxable amount is $42,600. This is our starting point.

Commence math journey...on the chart if you look at the first row, it says the tax rate is 10% and then you see a range. This means Madison gets the first $9,875 of her income taxed at 10%. Every dollar she earned up to $9,875 is taxed at 10%. Remember not every dollar is taxed the same amount.

This would be $987.50 so far (move the decimal over on $9,875.00). This amount is already calculated/included on the chart in the next row on the far right column.

But there is still $32,725 to be taxed. Only $9,875 has been taxed so far. If you look at the chart, once Madison's income gets to $9,876 it moves to the next rate or column which is 12%.

So, Madison will be taxed on every dollar in that range at the rate of 12% all the way up to $40,125.

To know exactly how much income was taxed at 12%, we subtract $9,875 (amount already accounted for) from $40,125 (the top amount in the bracket) and we get $30,250

$30,250 taxed at 12% is $3,630.

At this point she has $3,630 plus the $987.50 from the 10% rate, which puts her at $4,617.50 in income tax up to this point.

Again, the $4,617.50 is included on the chart on the following row in the far right column.

But since her taxable amount is $42,600 and only $40,125 has been accounted for, she moves into the *next* tax rate which is 22%

$42,600 (total taxable amount of her income) - $40,125 (money taxed already) = $2,475

$2,475 is taxed at 22% = $544.50

Now we have all the income accounted for.

$987.50 (amount taxed at 10%) + $3,630 (amount taxed at 12%) + $544.50 (amount taxed at 22%) = **$5,162**

Madison will pay approximately $5,162 in federal income taxes. This is a little over 9.5% of her income. Simply put, every $100 she makes about 10 dollars goes to the Federal Government.

This amount is called her **effective tax rate** because she is "effectively" paying 9.5%. Her **marginal tax rate** is 22% because her income puts her in that rate category *even though* only a small portion of her income was actually taxed at the level (22%).

Again, the example above only deals with Federal Income Tax.

If Madison works in a state with **State Income Tax**, then even more money is taxed. For instance, if Madison works in California, she also gets her money taxed. It doesn't matter if she has been taxed by the Federal government already, the State also taxes the same amount! Now the marginal tax rates are not as steep, but still substantial.

Here is a sample California Tax Chart:

TAX RATE	TAXABLE INCOME RANGE	TAX OWED
1%	$0 to $8,809	1% of taxable income
2%	$8,810 to $20,883	$88.09 plus 2% of the amount over $8,809
4%	$20,884 to $32,960	$329.57 plus 4% of the amount over $20,883
6%	$32,961 to $45,753	$812.65 plus 6% of the amount over $32,960
8%	$45,754 to $57,824	$1,580.23 plus 8% of the amount over $45,753

Without explaining the whole process again, you can look at the chart and see that she will be in the 8% marginal tax rate. There is a standard deduction as well but not as generous ($4,537).

All in all, Madison will pay in income tax:

Tax Type	Marginal Tax Rate	Effective Tax Rate	Taxes
Federal	22.00%	9.59%	$5,162
State	8.00%	3.56%	$1,957
Total Income Taxes			$7,119
Net Income After Taxes			$47,881

Ok, so only $47,881 is actually taken home out of the whole $55,000. But wait, there's more!

We haven't factored in *all* the taxes, just the regular income tax. The other areas your taxes are put to work are in are for programs such as **Social Security** and **Medicare**. You may also see on your paystub the letters **FICA**. This stands for **Federal Insurance Contributions Act** and this tax is deducted from each paycheck as well. As you work and pay FICA taxes, you contribute to Medicare and begin to earn credits for Social Security benefits.

Commence rabbit trail...

First, **Social Security**. The idea of Social Security is to help supplement incomes of the vulnerable and elderly. Social Security works like this: when you pay taxes into Social Security the tax money is used to pay benefits or supplement income for people in situations with one or more of the following:

- People who have already retired
- People who are disabled
- Survivors of deceased spouse workers
- Dependents (typically children) of beneficiaries

The money you pay in these taxes goes to people who receive benefits right now.

The unused money goes to a Social Security trust fund. As you work and pay taxes, you earn Social Security "credits." These credits determine *your* benefit if and when you choose to apply for Social Security benefits which are typically at retirement age (67 or older).

The nuances of Social Security are beyond the scope of an introduction, but just know you pay into this system and in theory will be able to benefit from this system at the appointed time. Not everyone gets the exact same amount of financial help, it is all based on your credits and life situation.

In order to associate and keep track of your eligibility and credits you are assigned a unique number which is cleverly named the **Social Security number** (SSN). If you are a citizen of the U.S., this is your livelihood. This number for most people is assigned at birth. It is critical you protect your unique social security number. Memorize the number, but do not carry your Social Security card around and do not write it down in a place where people could easily see it or steal it, do not keep it in your notes app. Keep the physical card in a safety deposit box.

As you will come to find, this number is used for purposes beyond Social Security. It is used to identify you for tax filing and documents like Passports and also to apply for loans whether its cars, houses, student loans, or even credit cards. With this in mind, you can see how someone with this number and a few other pieces of information easily scraped from the internet could allow them to steal your identity and money.

It is worth considering paying for a service to monitor and protect the usage of your Social Security number. If someone attempts to open a loan in your name or steal assets, these services are designed to stop the transaction and/or help recover the assets. Look up **Identity Theft Protection.**

Medicare

The other aspect of FICA is Medicare. Medicare is the federal health insurance program for those who are 65 or older. The Social Security credits you earn also count toward eligibility for Medicare when you reach age 65. There is more to the system, but as an introduction this is sufficient for now.

Returning back to taxes, this chart is a better reflection of how much Madison pays in taxes overall. With Madison's $55,000 income as a base, here is what she paid:

Tax Type	Marginal Tax Rate	Effective Tax Rate	Taxes
Federal	22.00%	9.59%	$5,162
FICA	7.65%	7.65%	$4,208
State	8.00%	3.56%	$1,957

Total Income Taxes		20.80%	$11,327
Income After Taxes			**$43,673**

Unemployment & Disability

The other tax category you may see on your pay stub is **SDI** or **SUI**. This stands for State Disability Insurance and State Unemployment Insurance. These taxes pay into an insurance fund intended to help those who have been furloughed, let go or fired from their job either due to financial reasons or disability. This money is meant to be a helping hand while someone looks for another job or fights through their disability. If you have been paying into the system, and you are let go from your job or disabled, you most likely will be able to file for unemployment and receive financial assistance as you look for another job.

A TAX STORY

Now that we know what we are up against, here is a user experience story of the whole process.

We will shift this time from Madison to her friend, Debbie. Debbie applies to work at Hot Dog on a Stick. The hourly wage is $15/hr. at "The Stick." After a flawless interview she is ready to churn lemonade and deep fry some corn dogs. Before she starts her new job she is given a form to fill out called a **W-4**[4].

You don't need to memorize this form number, but to help

---

4 https://www.irs.gov/pub/irs-pdf/fw4.pdf

explain it, the W stands for "withholding." Withholding essentially means "to take out." This form is asking you how much of *your* paycheck to *withhold* "W" or *take out* for "4" the government (that is not what W-4 actually stands for, it is just my pathetic remembering trick). To restate, how much withholding from your paycheck *for* (4) the government.

You may say, "oh, I get a choice? No thanks!"

We all wish it was tax optional.

The idea of this form is to make sure you are paying enough in taxes so that you won't have a big tax bill when you file your taxes in April every year. Conversely, you don't want to give too much because that means the government is holding onto your money, tax free! Interest you could have been earning on!

The W-4[5] form asks questions about other jobs or income you have. You are not required to report this information. The form can be overwhelming to look at, especially if it's your first time filling it out. But in most cases, you are fine just filling out Step 1 (your personal information) and then signing the form in Step 5. You only need to submit the first page to your employer.

If you later suspect that there is too much withholding or not enough, you may always complete an updated W-4 and write-in a specific amount in step 4.

If you are paying too much, then add an amount into the *deductions* box.

If you are not paying enough then you can add a specific amount

---

[5] https://www.irs.gov/pub/irs-pdf/fw9.pdf

to the *extra withholding* box.

Back to the story. Debbie gets her first paycheck or pay stub. This is a record or receipt of her earnings for that pay period. Usually, it is for a 2-week period, but it could be weekly or monthly. Every job is different.

She looks at her pay stub and is distraught. It says she only earned $640. She was about to storm into the office and complain to her manager, Karen, but she looked closer at her pay stub. Since she had worked 25 hours for two weeks, she was expecting $15 x 50 hours or $750.

What happened? She forgot about taxes. Her employer is required to withhold on her behalf. On her pay stub it says she did in fact work 50 hours and that her **gross pay** was in fact $750. (Again, gross is the total amount *before* any expenses or taxes or costs). Then she saw some items listed with a negative sign before the amount.

Federal Income Tax	$ -42
State Income Tax	$ -3
Social Security Tax	$ -47
Medicare Tax	$ -11
SUI/SDI	$ -8
NET Pay:	**$640**

Debbie then learned about those taxes (income, FICA, etc.) from Madison and she calmed down. She complained a little about "the government taking a big bite," but at least she understood her paycheck and can now budget properly. Her **net pay** or **net income** is the money she actually received. In accounting, **net** is really important because this is what is actually made or earned after all the taxes and expenses. So, when people quote their salary, it is not quite the whole story.

After a solid year of work, Debbie gets a form in the mail (or in her mailbox at work) in January. It is a **W-2 form**. This form is a "withholding" ("W" back to "2" you). Again, it doesn't mean that, it is just another pathetic mnemonic.

The W-2 is <u>not a form you complete</u>, rather more of a record of all the money made in the past year from that particular employer or business. The W-2 also shows how much was withheld and where it went in taxes or other areas. This is a really important document. You want to keep this! You will need it when you file your taxes in April (or earlier). If you have two jobs, you will get two W-2's.

Independent Workers, Self-Employment and Freelancers

If you do not work for a traditional business, but instead drive for Postmates or are a freelance photographer or graphic designer, you will not receive a W-4 and therefore you will not receive a W-2 at the end of the year. Don't worry, Christmas is still coming.

Because you technically work as a "contractor," you are required to complete a different form.

The form you get is called a **W-9**. (Sorry, no dumb remembering tricks here). This form is very basic. Your name, address, social security number and a signature is all that is needed. Companies hiring people for short term gigs or as a freelancer must issue this form because they need to report this information when they file *their* corporate taxes. They have to report what they paid you.

What you need to know is the company or person you are freelancing or contracting for does not withhold money from your check like we saw earlier. For example, if you are contracted to design a website for a company and you are quoted $2,500 for your work, you will get paid $2,500. Just because money wasn't withheld doesn't mean you are not responsible for taxes. You most definitely are. Even more responsible than if you worked for a traditional business.

Instead of getting a W-2, you receive a **1099**. The 1099 (like a W-2) shows/reports how much you received in compensation from the entity paying you. But here is where it gets weird and almost nobody tells you. You are responsible for making **estimated quarterly tax payments**. This means in addition to filing taxes in April, you are required to make tax payments four times a year!

"But wait," you say "I didn't get the 1099 thingy until January."

It doesn't matter, this is why it is called **estimated quarterly taxes**. You are supposed to estimate. And if you don't make these payments or you don't pay enough, there is a penalty levied on you based on your income, how much you underpaid and for how long you are late.

How much does one pay in quarterly taxes? Well, there are two taxes you pay just like a W-2 job. One is called the **self-employment tax** (this is also the FICA tax a.k.a. programs like Social Security and Medicare). This is 15.3% of your income. That breaks down specifically to 12.4% Social Security tax and 2.9% Medicare tax.

If you are paying attention, you may notice this amount for FICA tax is *higher* than the W-2 example for Debbie and for Madison. When you work for an employer you are only paying half. The employer pays the other half. That half is called **payroll taxes** for the employer.

Now before you cry foul on why some dude named Doug or a woman named Sheila in a corporate or traditional business setting pays less, they don't. You are allowed to write-off or deduct half the self-employment tax when you file in April. But you do need to pay the full amount for each quarterly payment.

The other tax you pay is income tax and is the same as the tax chart we looked at earlier. There are plenty of really good calculators online which can help you estimate your quarterly tax payment responsibility. These taxes can easily be paid online.

Also know, your state may also require quarterly tax payments so do not forget *both* Federal and State.

To plan, the recommendation is to set aside 30% of any paycheck to compensate for your taxes. You most likely won't pay all of it, but this is a conservative amount and a safe figure to work with.

A couple of other notes. It is possible to receive several 1099 forms and W-2 forms. Keep them all because you need all of them when you file your taxes (next section). You should also be aware; you may receive 1099s for other types of income that aren't work related. For instance, if you earn money from a savings account, you will receive a 1099 because the money you made on interest is taxable. If you won prize money at a Science Fair for your baking soda volcano, you will most likely be issued a 1099 for that prize money. In summary:

Form from employer: W-4 → Annual Report from employer: W-2

Form from entity paying: W-9 → Annual Report from entity: 1099

FILING TAXES

Even though some of your income has been going to the government, there is the annual tradition where you and the government settle accounts. The traditional date for this event is April 15th, but if it falls on a weekend then the date moves to Monday. The idea is to make sure each party got the exact amount of money they are supposed to get.

If you paid too much, you get a refund. While this seems great, this was your money to begin with. Our minds can trick us and we think this money is like finding $20 on the street. It isn't! This was your hard earned money that was being held by the government and now being returned to you. If this "refund" is really high, you withheld too much. You may want to adjust your W-4 at that point. If you are consumer savvy you will notice retailers encourage you to spend your refund with them. When stimulus checks were issued from the government due to Covid-19, the maximum amount was $1,200 and businesses like Costco strategically offered 82" 4K TV's for $1200 at the same time and many people went for it. Again, this is not a bonus or extra money, this is your money that was being held hostage so be careful about spending it as though Grandpa Joe kicked you a few C-notes for your birthday.

There is also a situation where you did not withhold enough. This means you owe money. This can be painful especially if you weren't planning or prepared to pay this tax bill, or you don't have the savings to cover it.

Certainly it is better to overpay than underpay, but the goal is to not owe or be owed anything. When this happens, it means you were getting the most out of your money.

When it is time to file taxes, you can hire a tax preparer. This is someone who will take care of the filing. But in most cases, you are just fine using an online software (TurboTax, H&R Block, etc.) If you make under a certain amount and do not have any other deductions or income streams, you may file for free[6].

If you use tax software, you will be prompted to enter your information from your W-2 or 1099 forms. The software walks you through each step and then calculates how much was withheld compared to how much you should have withheld based on your tax rate. If everything looks correct, you may file your taxes through the software program, meaning it submits your information to the IRS.

Earlier, we mentioned you are entitled to a standard deduction of $12,400 if you are not married but an individual income earner. In some cases, you may have more to deduct and if that is the case, you itemize your deductions. In general, **itemized deductions** are for expenses required for work, or donations to charity, or if you have kids to raise (also called dependents) because they are dependent on you.

You are required to list the specific deductions and amounts. It is important you have a record or receipt of these expenses. There is a government agency called the **IRS** (**Internal Revenue Service**) and they are like "tax cops." They exist to audit (check) tax returns to make sure people are not lying or exaggerating their deductions or under reporting their income. There are also

[6] https://apps.irs.gov/app/freeFile/browse-all-offers

people who do not file or pay taxes at all and they are definitely on the hunt for these people. Don't be these people.

It is beyond the scope here to discuss all the tax laws, loopholes and things that are deductible, so either look it up online or talk to a tax professional or a **CPA** (Certified Public Accountant).

Up to this point we have examined how there are some "forces" working against you by default in the background: time, inflation, and taxes. If you do not make a conscious effort, these forces act against you. There is another force which can team up with those others and act against you as well if you aren't careful, debt.

DEBT

Debt is spending money you don't have. Debt is the exact opposite of freedom. Debt means always being in a state of owing. It weighs heavy on you. It promises happiness or eventual profit in the future if you will just sacrifice the present. Debt is very easy to get into and impossibly hard to get out of. One of the core tenets of learning personal finance is to avoid unhealthy debt.

Credit cards

You may have seen or heard all sorts of commercials for credit cards. The commercials usually focus on all the perks and things like "cash back" you get for using them. Sounds appealing. Some cards just look really cool and you imagine yourself flexing it at Cheesecake Factory. But a good way to think of credit cards is to think of them like a campfire. If you know how to use fire and are cautious, it really adds to your camping experience. If you are careless or do not know how to contain and control a campfire it gets out of control and can destroy your campsite and property.

Here is a basic definition: a credit card is a card you apply for and is backed (funded) by a bank extending you "a line of credit." A line of **credit** is a predetermined amount of money (sometimes called the **spending limit**) you are permitted to borrow. In its most simple form, when you use a credit card, you are borrowing money from the bank to make your purchase. The bank pays the merchant for the item or meal, and then you pay back the bank or credit card company.

Credit and credit card offers may come in all sorts of places and forms. You may get a direct mail offer. This means a piece of physical mail comes to you with your name on it and says "You're Pre-Approved!"

Sounds great. Who doesn't like being approved?

Another place you might get offers are at retail stores. Many times the person who rings you up at the register will give an offer like, "sir, would you like to open up a total rewards credit card? If you open it today (apply & get approved) you can take 20% off your first purchase!" Other times you may be at a sporting event or on a college campus and see a booth with free merchandise to take if you sign up for a card.

And of course, if you see Samuel L. Jackson hawking a card you like, you can always apply yourself online.

So why are these potentially dangerous? First, if you don't have the discipline, this money costs way too much to borrow. For some reason, people view it as free money, but it's actually some of the most expensive money out there. It is also wise to not regard a credit card as an emergency fund. You want to build up your own emergency fund for that purpose.

Quick reset on types of cards: **a debit card** is money from your checking account and a **credit card** is money borrowed from a bank or credit card company. It is possible to have both from the same bank, the difference lies in from where the money comes.

What are the benefits of a credit card?

To begin with, there is the convenience factor. Purchases are easily made and many merchants are used to card payments.

Another benefit is that since you are borrowing the bank's

money, if there is a fraudulent purchase they are very good with closing the card, getting the money back and issuing you a brand new card immediately.

Many cards also offer perks and benefits. These might be in the form of points you can trade in for gifts, products, travel expenses or airline miles. It might also come in the form of "cash back." Meaning for every X amount of dollars you spend, the card will issue cash back to you as a reward.

On the surface it sounds like an adult Chuck E. Cheese, spend money and get prizes! But like Chuck's cross-selling, there are other ways they make money.

Some cards with very lucrative perks and benefits typically require an annual fee. This means you have to pay a certain amount every year just to use the card. This could range from $50 a year to $550 a year. Many of these types of cards offer enough perks that if you leverage all of the benefits then it may cover and exceed the fee you paid.

For instance, you may get a perk for a travel credit up to a certain amount of money. This is where any travel related expenses (hotel, airfare, parking) are reimbursed up to a certain amount. You may also get free access to airport lounges or discounts on some services. Some cards offer free or discounted Uber or Lyft or other services.

There is a subculture of people who analyze and try to leverage the most out of these cards. Feel free to lurk online, but this is definitely an advanced player move. Only if you have proven the discipline and have the money to pay for purchases should you engage in making the most of these cards. Not all cards are created equal so you need to do your research. More on what to look for a little later.

Finally, another benefit to a credit card is a chance to build "credit."

Credit/Credit Scores

You may have heard phrases like "I need to build my credit" or "I have bad credit" or maybe you hear an advertisement to "increase your credit score." A **credit score** is a score to determine how likely a borrower is to pay money back.

For a long time, colleges and universities have used standardized tests like the SAT and ACT as one form of measuring the likelihood of a potential applicant being successful at their school. It isn't the only metric, but it is a quick way to determine whether or not to consider a student for admission.

Credit Scores have a similar concept. If you want to take out a loan, or apply for a credit card, or rent an apartment, the bank, business, or person taking the risk on you by loaning you money are all wondering how likely you are to pay it back. They can "check" or "run" your credit to see how well you score.

Some credit checks or reports are very thorough and some are simple. If you get an offer for a credit card because you are "pre-approved," then that means a simple or "soft" credit check was made to determine your risk. The "hard" or serious credit checks are when bigger purchases or loans are being considered. These checks can have an impact on your score. More on this later.

A thorough credit check or report includes your entire payment history for the last 7-10 years! Any payment missed or late is reflected. They know everything. Credit checks/reports show

how many credit cards you have opened in the past or are currently open and when you opened them. They know if you have a car loan, and how many payments you've made. How much you still owe on any loan you have, etc.

With all of this information, a company called **FICO** (the acronym stands for Fair, Isaac and Company, but everyone knows it as FICO) came up with a scoring system to calculate your payment history and information into a simple score. Similar to how your answering questions on an SAT produces a score. There are others, but FICO is the most well known. And while not every business or bank uses the FICO score, most do.

FICO Score Levels

In the graphic below you can see the different credit levels based on score. Again, your approval for loans and or the interest rate (cost to borrow the money) you get are dependent on these scores. Obviously being above 700 is reflective of good credit.

How FICO Scores Are Weighted or Calculated

The graphic below shows how the score is weighted and calculated. Clearly, having a history of making payments on time make up a huge part of your score.

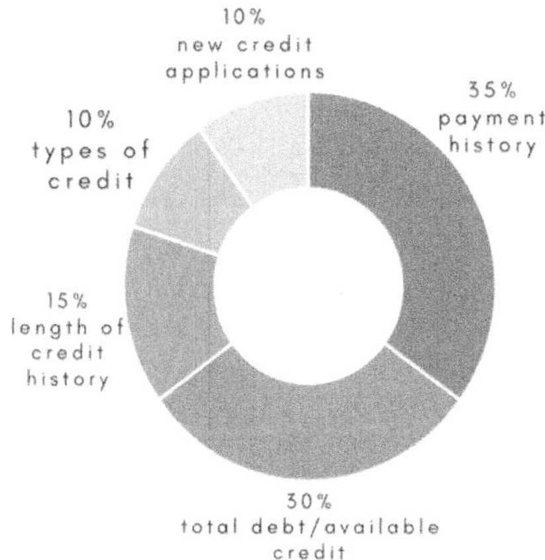

What to look for in a Credit Card

The assumption at this point is you are disciplined and have focused on building an emergency fund first. You understand the difference between wants and needs. The other assumption is you are in a position to pay off your card on time, every month. If those are indeed true of you, then here are some things to look for in a credit card.

Credit Card issuers have to give you all the information and details about the card, so it is up to you to look for some key things. To make it easier, issuers have to include what is called a Schumer Box. The Schumer Box is similar to those nutrition facts labels you see on packaged food. This is to make it easier and more clear on the terms of the card. The Schumer Box is not perfect nor does it explain everything, but it is certainly where to start.

Example "Schumer Box"

Interest Rates and Interest Charges	
Annual Percentage Rate (APR) for Purchases	**10.99%** to **21.99%** when you open your account, based on your creditworthiness. After that, this APR will vary with the market based on the Prime Rate.
How to Avoid Paying Interest on Purchases	Your due date is at least 28 days after the close of each billing cycle. We will not charge you any interest on purchases if you pay your entire balance (adjusted for any financing plan) by the due date each month.
For Credit Card Tips from the Consumer Financial Protection Bureau	To learn more about factors to consider when applying for or using a credit card, visit the website of the Consumer Financial Protection Bureau at **https://www.consumerfinance.gov/learnmore**

Fees	
Annual Fee	$150
Transaction Fees	None
Penalty Fees	None
Other Fees	None

HOW WE WILL CALCULATE YOUR BALANCE:
We use the daily balance method (including new Transactions).

First, you want to determine if there is a fee or **annual fee** to use the card. Again, this is an advanced player move with lots of benefits and perks to leverage, so if you are looking to get your first card ignore these annual fee cards for now.

Then look at the **APR**. APR is the "annual percentage rate" or the interest you are being charged to borrow money. The reason it is called annual is because that is the basis for how the interest is calculated. But this doesn't mean you are only charged interest once a year, it means it determines your interest rate for the year.

In other words, the rate may be based on an annual basis, but the calculation is performed daily. Let's say you owe or have a balance of $5,000 on your card. And let's assume the published APR is 14%.

The calculation would be 14/365 ("APR" divided by "days in 1 year"). In this case, 14/365 = 0.038. This figure is then multiplied by your current balance, in this case $5,000.

So, $5000 X 0.038 = $1.92 a day

If you make no other purchases in that month, you will see a new **balance** (the updated amount you owe) on your statement of $5057.60

$1.92 (daily rate) x 30 days = $57.60 plus the $5,000 you owe.

The APR is almost always a range (something like 14% - 28%) and oftentimes includes the word "variable." This means that the interest you pay to borrow money is not fixed—it may not stay at the same rate. The rate could change at any time for any reason. Sometimes, a card may start with 0% for a short period to get you to sign up and then it balloons to 18% after a year. Be careful.

APR or interest rates don't change arbitrarily or randomly, there is usually a trigger that would cause it to change. The main trigger being a missed or late payment. You could apply and be approved for a credit card at 18% APR. If you missed just one payment or are late, it could shoot up to 24% or higher! It all depends on the terms, so read them. Not all cards are created equal.

Regardless whether the card says 18% or 28%, this is expensive money to borrow. This is why it is important to make sure you can pay it off. The other aspect to look for is the "grace period" or "due date." This is how many days you are allowed to pay off the money without being charged interest.

But this can be misleading because if your grace period is 25 days and you pay on the 26th day, it doesn't mean you are charged interest on 1 day. You are charged interest for the last 26 days!

The grace period can range from 21 days to 28 days. This can be hard to track if you make a lot of purchases because you are only given a statement every month. You aren't shown which items are late or from a previous period. When you make a payment, the money is applied to the oldest purchase.

The credit card bill statement then gives an option to make a minimum payment (which is shown) or to pay off the entire balance.

The minimum payment is typically a percentage of your total balance or what you owe.

Another fee to look for in the terms is a "**late fee**." If you are late on a payment, you can be hit with a fee on top of the interest. Ouch. Here is where some people who are not disciplined can get into trouble. Storytime:

Don Flamenco applied for a credit card and was given a credit limit of $10,000. This means he has the access to borrow up to $10,000. His APR is 24% and the grace period is 21 days. Don saw an ad for a new iMac computer and all-in with taxes would be $5,555.55

He doesn't need it, but he wants it. So he goes to Best Buy to get this computer. As he checks out, ready to use his new card the cashier in a nice blue polo and khakis says, "if you open up a Best Buy credit card today, you can get 10% off right now!" Don will feel less guilty about this expensive purchase if he got a deal, so he agrees.

He uses his new Best Buy card and *voila* a new computer...and a $5000 balance on his Best Buy card. Don gets his first credit card statement and sees the option to make a minimum payment. The amount listed is $100 (this is 2% of the balance, or 2% of what he owes).

He thinks, "this is easy, all I have to do is pay $100 a month?!" Don thinks he is clever and sets up auto pay for $100 every month. He sets it and forgets it. The problem is that Don forgot that his APR is 14%. If Don does not address this, he will have to pay $100 a month for, wait for it...the next 302 months in order to pay this debt off. That is about 25 years!

Not only that, because of the interest on the purchase, when he finally pays it off he will have paid over $11,000 for a $5,000 purchase!

You can see how quickly in a hole you can get yourself into, especially if you are unable to make payments.

One other note about Credit Cards. With credit cards you are also able to get "**cash advances**." This is where instead of having the bank essentially buy the item for you and you pay them back, you are able to withdraw a certain amount of cash with your credit card. The APR on cash advances are always significantly higher. Do not even consider this option even though credit cards will offer this and state the APR for cash advances.

While there are lots of frustrations about how education is delivered, one thing school does teach you is that if you are late or you fail to turn in an assignment, a grade of zero is very detrimental and difficult to dig out of. The reason is the range for a fail is 0-59.9. If you labored to get half of your points back, you are still failing. Paying off debts are similar. A missed or late payment can set you back and make it incredibly difficult to catch up.

One other point to mention. You are able to opt-in, meaning you have to make the choice to set up for auto-pay. Auto Pay is a feature which will automatically pull the minimum amount due on your credit card from a checking account or whatever account you select. This should be set up right away. While it does not protect you from interest payments, it does protect you from a missed/late payment, a "hit" against your credit, a potential fee, and an increase in APR. Just do it.

If you are in a position to get your first credit card, one recommendation is to go to your current bank. The bank already has a relationship with you and may be more likely to approve you for a card even if you have no credit to your name. This is a great "training wheels" option because you can link your bank account to your credit card and set up auto pay. You can see everything in one app and you can start with a low credit limit. For instance, if you are worried about your discipline, then set the credit limit to a small amount. Once you start to prove yourself you can handle credit cards, you can either ask to increase the credit limit or consider a different card. Credit score gurus would recommend you do not close that card, but pay off the whole balance and never touch it or use it. The reason is that your score suggests you have more credit extended to you that you can handle.

Point of Sale Loans

Another way to finance or "borrow money" for a purchase is through something called **point of sale loans**. Here is how they work:

Imagine you are looking to buy a new hydroponics kit online. You don't have the money to buy it outright, but for sake of argument let's say it is a legitimate need and not a want. So you add the hydroponics kit to your online cart and see some options to pay for it.

You could use a credit card, Apple Pay or Google Pay, PayPal OR you have an option for a loan from a 3rd party[7]. This 3rd party is offering to essentially buy the kit for you and you pay them back in nice divided up monthly payments. This could be a better option since many times, they offer a rate close to or at 0% to borrow. It does depend on a quick credit check. The danger is tricking yourself into thinking you can afford the monthly payments when you really cannot. There can be fees and expenses that you can get hit with. (Another reason why a budget is your friend). You will see more and more of this option not only online but also in physical retail stores. Even Credit Card companies are beginning to offer these as well.

Merchant Service Fees

One aspect consumers don't see regarding credit cards, but has an impact on them are **merchant services fees**. When you use your credit card or debit card at a store or restaurant or even online, there are fees to process the transaction. You may even have been at a location where they will not let you use a card

[7] Afterpay and Affirm are some current companies offering this.

unless you spend a certain amount of money. The reason the merchant won't accept your card is because the merchant loses too much money on the transaction.

To explain: If you look at a credit card you will see the bank name on it like Chase, Bank of America, Citi, Capital One, etc. Sometimes it may be an airline or a retail store, but they are always backed by a bank. You will also see a small logo with MasterCard or Visa on it.

The process goes like this. You present your card at a restaurant. The restaurant swipes or inserts the card into a machine. The restaurant pays a percentage of each sale to use the machine. The machine is what connects to a network (Visa, MasterCard) and the network "talks" to the bank with your credit card number to make sure there is enough credit and communicates the transaction.

Since the bank is paying the merchant in a timely manner, they also charge the merchant for their card being used. You may have seen a couple other card options out there like American Express and Discover. These companies also issue cards with the ability to borrow money, but there is a slight difference in their structure. They are both the "bank" and the "network." They can partner with banks and just do the "network" part, or partner with businesses and do both. But this is why they are different and they tend to be a little more expensive for transactions.

Depending on *how* the card is transacted can cost more to the merchant as well. A typed in card number has a higher likelihood of fraud, or being a stolen credit card as opposed to a more secure chip. The bank factors in the risk into the payment. A card swipe is a little less risky and as mentioned the chip is least risky.

Also, all those cool perks you get and cash back and points are not free. Someone pays for them and it is usually the merchant.

In summary, the credit card processing costs a fee and is passed onto the merchant or seller. This is typically in the range of 2-3% plus a transaction fee. If you have tried to sell something online you may have noticed this. If you were to sell a $100 jacket on your e-commerce site, you will get charged approximately 2.9% + .30 cents (more or less). If you do the math, this means you will not receive $100, but around $96.75. For one transaction it may not seem much. But if you repeat this transaction multiple times you can see how much potential income is lost.

Therefore many merchants and businesses build this into their price, which falls back onto you.

Have fun exploring this world.

To shift away from consumer debt, let's quickly look at another major debt for many Americans.

BRIEF NOTE ON STUDENT LOANS

An assumption is being made that the reader is familiar with FAFSA and the basic process of applying for student loan aid. On the topic of debt, this is burdensome. Check out these student loan statistics[8]:

Student loan debt in the US = $1.68 trillion

Average debt is $37,584

---

[8] https://educationdata.org/student-loan-debt-statistics

44.7 million student borrowers are in debt

2.4 million borrowers owe an average of $48,819 each in private loans

Average borrowing cost for a bachelor's degree is $30,030

If you are considering college, be mindful of where you source your loans. Private loans may seem like a good idea, but they can be dangerous. Try to stick to these Federal Loans first if you can.

Direct Subsidized Stafford Loans

Students with exceptional financial need can apply for these loans. The subsidy or help is that students do not have to pay interest on their principal taken out during their schooling or six months after they complete or leave school (grace period). The U.S Department of Education or more accurately taxpayers pays the interest for them, but after those six months, the interest begins. The 2019-2020 Interest Rate for Direct Subsidized Stafford Loans was 4.53% and if you are able to qualify for this loan, this is the best deal. There is a limit, but you can look these up.

Direct Unsubsidized Stafford Loans

In this case, these student borrowers do not need to demonstrate financial need, they also pay interest on their loans from the moment that they take the loan out. The 2019-2020 Interest Rate was 4.53% for undergraduates and 6.08% for graduate or professional students.

The point of this section is to take seriously the decision of education and the burden of debt when you graduate. There is no shame whatsoever to knock out as many credits as you can at a

Community College and finish at a University. If you value the full 4-5 year experience, then start to make plans on how to reduce your debt burden when you graduate.

A good number to shoot for the whole 4 year undergraduate education is to not borrow beyond your expected starting salary your first year out of school. So if you expect $65,000 your first year out of school, then do not borrow more than that for the full four years.

What happens if I do find myself in debt?

The hope of this book would be that if you are not currently in debt, you would work hard to keep it that way. But life happens sometimes, or you took on student loan debt. There are a few options to consider.

If you are in a terrible situation, you may be able to use a service which negotiates your debt. But this also comes with a cost.

Consolidation could be another option. Debt consolidation is where you pool your debts into one pile and get a set interest rate typically better than what you had prior. The issue is that while you may be pleased to see a lower interest rate, it is only low because the payment length has been extended. You end up paying more in the long run. Sometimes you are required to offer collateral or assets or things you own in order to get this privilege. If you fail to make your repayments, the company that issues your loan can take some or all of your property. This is called a **secured loan** because there is some "security" in knowing your assets can be seized in case you cannot pay. So be careful!

But if you can be patient, you can start to reduce debt with the "snowball method." The idea is to not get overwhelmed with all the debt, but start paying off what you can. This is more of a psychological method. It may not be the absolute best in terms of math, but it addresses the issue many people struggle with and that is being so overwhelmed they don't act. With a snowball method you are making progress and it inspires more progress. The method is to start with the smallest debts first and then move to the bigger ones. With persistence you can get yourself out of debt and like a snowball becoming an avalanche you can tackle the monster that is your debt.

Whatever you do, avoid the temptation of predatory loans such as **payday loans** or **auto-title loans**. Payday loans promise you cash today before you get your paycheck. The interest rates on these loans are atrocious and unfortunately for most, this quick up-front cash actually creates bigger debt for consumers and can keep them in a cycle of giving a majority of their paycheck to these loans. Auto-title loans use your car as a basis for the loan. They charge enormous interest and can take your car. In some cases, you even get penalized for paying off the loan early!

It is worth repeating that a budget would be necessary to help work through this.

INVESTING

This is the section you are most likely here for. How to make more money with your money with securities. **Securities** are tradable financial instruments. Either in the form of equity (stocks or ownership of a business), debt (bonds), a combination of the two, or derivatives of a security (options).

Disclaimer: this isn't a how-to but rather an overview of some investment vehicles (or investment opportunities) available and how they work. There is always risk involved. You must be prepared to lose money on any investment.

STONKS! INVESTING IN THE STOCK MARKET

If you have seen Shark Tank, you know that a small business pitches their idea or company to the Sharks for money and mentorship in exchange for part equity in the company. **Equity** means ownership. So you will hear almost every pitch begin with something along the lines of "I am asking for $100,000 in exchange for 20%." Then the Sharks scribble notes on their legal pads.

The entrepreneurs in this case are offering up 20% ownership of their business in exchange for cash to help grow the business. They are essentially selling off a piece of the business. The

valuation is based on what someone is willing to pay for a share or ownership.

To simplify, if I have a whole pizza with 10 slices and someone is willing to pay me $2 for a slice, this values my pizza at $20. 10 slices x $2 (highest amount someone is willing to offer for it) = $20.

In the Shark Tank example, the small startup company says "we will sell ⅕ of our business or a 20% slice for $100,000." This means they value the business at $500,000

The math is $100,000 / .20

This does not mean they have $500,000 in revenue, or that they will even make that much any time soon.

There is an assumption that the company will grow and be worth at least that amount based on how they have been doing so far and/or based on how the market values products similar to it.

The Shark is willing to take a risk and give the $100,000 now because if that startup company grows in value and someone wants to pay $5 Million for the whole pie or business down the road, this means the Shark grew their investment slice from $100,000 to $1 Million!

For those who like percentages, that is a 900% return on investment! (Just a little bit better than that Savings account).

Now of course, this is all on paper. The Shark would have to sell their share in the business to get the money. And then of course, get taxed on it.

With this understanding we can start to talk about stocks. Stocks are also equity or shares or ownership of a business. But instead of going on Shark Tank, a more mature company can choose to "go public." This is another way to raise money for the company as well as increase the investment of all those who invested money early on (just like the Shark).

So let's say a company wants to raise money so they can grow and build and hire and advertise to the level they need to in order to be more successful. The company would go through the process to get listed on a Stock Exchange. There are ways to go unlisted which are beyond our scope.

Another popular method of going public is through **SPAC**'s which stands for **special purpose acquisition company**. Very simply put, SPAC's are shell companies which exist and are publicly traded, but don't do anything, sell anything or make money. They exist to raise money with the goal of merging with a company desiring to go public. The public can invest in these SPAC's, but the unknown is if and when a merger takes place and if it'll be successful. It is a much quicker process for companies to go public with SPAC's than a traditional listing which can take 12-18 months. Virgin Galactic and DraftKings are a couple of examples of companies going public via SPAC. SPACs are interesting so certainly worth a deep dive.

Most common for businesses is to list on a known Exchange like the **New York Stock Exchange** (NYSE) or the National Association of Securities Dealers Automated Quotations **(NASDAQ).**

There are other exchanges as well but these two are the most well known and biggest stock exchanges in the United States. A company must go through some regulatory hoops, one of them is issuing an **S-1 form** for the public to inspect. The S-1 form gives an overview of the company: why they are going public and objectives for the money received by selling shares, future risks etc. Once approved, a date is set for the company to go "public." This is the company's **Initial Public Offering** or **IPO**.

A valuation is assessed and then the IPO price is set. This is the opening price to buy shares of the company IPO. The company sells those IPO shares and with the massive influx of cash can go about growing their business. There is more detail in the background, but this is the big picture.

Those shares are either held by investors (big or small) in the hope the shares grow or they sell after a small gain. If you were to buy a share of Snapchat (SNAP) today, the share you are buying was at one time an IPO share. Someone else or multiple people owned that share before you. Companies can issue secondary shares later on and it does occur but is rare.

The value or price listed for that share is what people are willing to buy or sell the share for.

IPO's can be seen as an opportunity to get in early with a company with the hope they grow in value to be sold later for profit. For example, an IPO share of Amazon back in 1997 cost $18. If you bought $1,000 worth and held until today, you would have over 2 Million dollars in Amazon shares!

To recap, when you buy a share or stock of a company you are typically buying an old IPO share. This doesn't change the importance of the share because whether you buy it as an IPO or 20 years later, either way you are buying ownership rights in a company.

With this ownership you are given the ability to vote for certain business decisions. Of course for most people, it is about the investment. And usually the better the business does, the better you do. But that is one other thing to talk about. You see, a business could report great news in terms of revenue for the past quarter but that doesn't mean your shares go up in value. The share or stock you own is only as valuable as the "market" or people interested in buying the stock are willing to pay for it.

While we're here, it is also worth noting that the economy is not the same as the stock market. Though they often inform one another, they are not always in sync.

Quarterly Reports

Every quarter (every 3 months) companies will have earnings calls or reports. This means they share how well the company has performed in the last quarter in terms of revenue or losses and what they expect for the next quarter and beyond. There are a couple metrics investors look at (more on that later), but these reports help gauge the health of the company, their future, and can have an impact on share price.

Stock Tables and Basic Metrics

When you look up a company to invest in or see the performance of a stock, there is so much data and information available to you. Just like in sports, there are stats on players, trends and percentages.

Here is a walkthrough on the basic information you will see listed, some of which are reported during earnings calls, and what it all means.

As always, you can dig even deeper and find even more detailed metrics, charts and graphs, but we will start with some basics.

Let's take a look at a fake company. You heard a stock tip from your cool cousin about the company, RATT and so you go online to your favorite finance website and type in RATT. Let's break down what you will see:

RATT

Really Awesome Tik Toks, Inc.

218.64 -1.07 (-0.49%)

The "symbol" or "ticker" for the company is shortened to make it easy to remember, track, buy/sell and lookup. In this case the company's ticker or symbol is **RATT**. It represents the fake company Really Awesome Tik Toks Incorporated.

Most of the time you will also see the full company name listed. This is important to check if you have not bought this company before. Sometimes, there are symbols or tickers which seem correct, but are not. For instance, Zoom (as in Zoom calls, Zoom bombing, Zoom background and Zoom University) has the ticker **ZM**. There was another small foreign company listed on the stock exchange when Zoom was gaining popularity that had the ticker symbol ZOOM. Guess what happened? People bought the wrong Zoom stock because they didn't double check. So make sure you know what you are getting.

Now for those numbers. The 218.64 represents the current market price for a share of RATT or $218.64 a share.

The -1.07 which you will usually see in either green or red (green means positive and would be +1.07; red means negative or "down" and is -1.07). Looking at the info above, it appears

RATT is down -1.07 or $1.07 from the most recent trading day.

Then the change is also listed in terms of percentage. RATT is down -0.49% from last trading day.

This chart below is more of a reference guide/glossary. Most websites display data in cleaner fashion. Nonetheless, take a look below to learn about the different metrics of a stock chart and stock data. We will stick with our example of RATT.

RATT

Really Awesome Tik Toks, Inc.

218.64 | -1.07 | (-0.49%) |

Previous Close	219.71	This is the price ($219.71) which our stock RATT closed at the previous trading day.
Open	219.98	This is the market price for one share of RATT when the market opened for the day. You will notice it is different from the close by a little bit. This is because there are transactions taking place even when the market is closed for you.
Bid	219.62	The **BID** is the current price an investor is willing to pay for a share. (If you buy as a "market order" aka the current price you will pay the *ASK* price (below) not the BID price)
Ask	219.72	The **ASK** is the current price a seller of the share is asking or wants to sell

		at. Note: there is a difference between the two prices. This is known as the "spread."
Days Range	218.38 - 220.59	This is the range of prices for the day. You can see that 218.38 was the lowest price paid for a share, and 220.59 was the highest price paid for a share.
52 Week Range	124.23 - 231.91	This is the range for the previous year, measured in weeks. You can see RATT was trading at 124.23 at its lowest and 231.91 at its highest. Compared to today's price, you can see where it sits in the range.
Volume	2,234,480	Volume represents the amount of shares traded during this trading day.
Avg. Volume	2,984,675	This is the average amount of shares traded usually calculated from the previous twelve months.
Market Cap	163.023B	This is the capitalization or the value of the company. This is calculated by taking the amount of shares "outstanding" or shares investors can purchase and multiplying it by the current share price. Remember our analogy of a pizza slice. If I have a pizza with 10 slices and you are willing to pay $5 for slice, the "market cap" and of the pizza is now $50 (10 slices or shares x $5)

PE Ratio	33.38	This metric is called the **Price/Earnings Ratio**. This is the price you are paying for shares based on how much the company earns. This is calculated by taking the current share price divided by the EPS (below). The lower the P/E ratio, the less you are paying for the same past earnings. If the P/E is high, it suggests investors are willing to pay more and are anticipating future growth down the road.
EPS	6.55	The EPS or **earnings per share** indicates the profitability of RATT. It is calculated by taking the net income of the company and dividing it by the total number of outstanding shares (shares available to buy and sell on the market). This means RATT is earning a net income of $6.55 for every share out there. Some companies have a negative EPS. This means they are not profitable yet. When companies release their quarterly reports, this figure is used by investors and analysts to determine if the company is doing better or worse than projected.
Dividend & Yield	5.16 (2.35%)	Some companies which are more established reward investors (technically part owners, albeit very small) with **dividends**. Think of

		dividends as a form of profit sharing. The company distributes some of the profits with investors. In our case, RATT is paying $5.16 for every share you own. This means every 3 months you will get $5.16 for every share you own. You can choose to take the money (taxable) or you can choose to "reinvest dividends" which means that dividend money goes to buying more shares or partial shares of RATT. The **yield** is what you are getting based on what you pay. In this case, 5.16 (dividend) / 218.64 (current price) is a 2.35% yield. To simplify, you are making over 2% on your investment. If you look up a company and this is blank or "N/A" it means they do not currently issue dividends.
Ex-Dividend Date	Nov 30, 2020	Dividends are paid out quarterly (every 3 months). The amount is set by the board of directors as well as the date the dividends are issued. This date listed here means that this is the last day to purchase a share (or more shares) in order to be included in the dividend payment.

There are several theories and methods to determine when to buy stock or determine if it is overvalued or not. There are endless charts, graphs and metrics to look at in order to analyze a company's value and also examine trends based on charts.

A breakdown of each of these is beyond our scope, but all of this information is certainly available on your favorite finance website. Yahoo Finance is highly regarded. The main thing to keep in mind is there is no magic metric. Just as you cannot evaluate the talent of an athlete based on one stat, you cannot evaluate or make an informed decision on one measurement. You may see posts of "just look at this metric" or "follow that chart," but remember the market is more complex than one stat. And the stock market is not the economy. It is more reflective of human behavior.

ETF's & Mutual Funds

You have probably heard the phrase, "don't put all your eggs in one basket." The idea is to spread out the risk. If you leave your eggs in one basket and they are stolen or snacked on by a wild animal, you lose everything. The same philosophy can be applied to investing. Putting all your investment into one company is risky. So while you can choose to invest in a bunch of different companies, there are also ways to spread out the risk (or diversify) or get exposure to many different sectors by investing in funds.

Funds are essentially a collection or basket of different stocks or other equities (owning pieces of something) pooled together and sold as shares or slices. Let's start with Mutual Funds.

Mutual Funds

To get a sense of Mutual Funds, I will give two different analogies. Let's say your friend Katie is a Pokémon card expert. Katie approaches you and some other people and says, "if you each give me money, I will pool it together and buy the best cards which I think will best grow in value. And as they grow in value, you each get a percentage of the total value based on the amount you paid me. If you want to redeem your portion, you will get cash for your share or percentage of the investment."

This is a basic and simplified concept of how a mutual fund works: you put your money in with other people's money, and the expert (Katie or whoever) chooses what to invest or buy with the goal of benefiting everyone.

To get another sense of how mutual funds work, let's talk pizza (again). When you order a pizza with multiple toppings, the toppings are spread out across the whole pizza. When you grab a slice of this loaded pizza you get "exposure" to *all* the different toppings on your one slice. If you go to a pizza joint for a slice, you are paying for a portion of the whole pizza. A whole pizza might be $20 and with 10 slices cut, you buy a slice for $2. You get exposure to all the toppings but in a convenient and reasonably priced slice.

So a mutual fund is where a selection of stocks are pooled together into a single fund and an investor (you and me) can buy a share or "slice" of that fund. A mutual fund manager (similar to Katie the Pokémon expert) has an objective with the fund. It might be to invest in specific types of stock (growth, dividend, etc.) or sectors of stock (tech, energy, etc.) The mutual fund manager therefore has a strategy of moving shares and stock in and out of the fund.

The fund could also include other equities like bonds and cash, etc. but we will stick to stocks for now. When you buy a slice or share of the fund, you get a piece of all those stocks from the fund. The idea is to allow you to get exposure or investment in *multiple* stocks. This way, if one company goes bad for some reason, you reduce risk because there are plenty other stocks keeping the fund healthy. Think of it as "strength in numbers."

A key difference of Mutual Funds compared to stocks is that Mutual Funds are not bought and sold throughout the market day. Instead, as the assets or stocks move in price throughout the day, the fund then re-calculates the value at market close. Most mutual funds execute trades once per day after the close of the market. So if you want to buy or sell a share of a mutual fund, it will occur at the market close *after* the value has been settled for the day.

In terms of knowing what to look for in a Mutual Fund, if you remember how a stock has a specific ticker or symbol, the same goes for Mutual Funds. There is also basic information listed to know the price and performance of the fund.

Here is an example with another fake Mutual Fund, **CROWX** and all the basic information to look at.

NAV / 1-Day Return	17.36 / 0.99 %	NAV means "**Net Asset Value**." This is the amount of the total value of all the assets in the fund *divided by* the shares available for buying and selling on the market. The NAV is also the price to buy 1 slice of this fund. In this case it is $17.36 and

		is up almost 1% from last trading day.
Total Assets	124.8 Bil.	The total value of the assets or stock in the fund is 124.8 Billion dollars.
Expense Ratio	0.850%	This is REALLY IMPORTANT. This is how much it costs you for the mutual fund company to operate the fund. If you bought $10,000 of CROWX and it had a 5% return at the end of the year, that would be $10,500. BUT with the **expense ratio**, what you actually get is $10,415. This may not seem like that much of a loss, but this number compounds. (see chart below)
Fee Level	Average	Beyond the expense ratio can also be fees. These can include sales charges (a.k.a. commissions), redemption fees, transaction fees, and other maintenance fees. In this case, the fee level is "average" which means some fees do exist and are typical compared to other funds.
Category	US Fund Large Growth	The category is a general way to label the fund. This is a fund consisting of investing in

		companies in the United States (US) which have stocks with room for continued growth (Large Growth).
Investmen t Style	Large Growth	The investment style is also the objective. In this case, the fund is attempting to achieve growth.
Longest Manager Tenure	21 years	We talked about fund managers who make decisions on what to include and what to sell in the fund. This lets you know how many years the longest serving manager has been managing the fund.
Status	Open	There are two types of Mutual Funds: **Open and Closed**, but for our purposes open-ended is a typical Mutual Fund and what you would interact with the most. An Open fund means there is no limit to how many shares are created. A Closed-end fund is structured a little different and has a set amount of shares.
TTM Yield	0	The TTM means Trailing Twelve Months which makes a calculation based on the last 12 months of performance. If this

		fund contained dividends, then this would show the yield you are getting out of each slice or share. This fund doesn't so it is 0 or N/A.
Turnover	26%	This is a percentage of how many equities or stocks in the fund get changed in and out (turned over or frequency of buying and selling). If you are looking for something more long-term and steady, this number should be lower.
Min. Investmen t	$2500	This is the amount of money required to get into the fund. Sometimes this number is 0, sometimes this number is massive (in the millions).

To get a sense of actual returns, by using the information above and with that expense ratio of .85% take a look at the chart below. We will assume a young person who has $25,000 invested in CROWX and adds $10,000 to the fund every year, while earning a 5% average annual return.

# of years invested	**Fund Value on 5% return, no fees/expense**	**Portfolio value lost to expense ratio (.85%)**	**After-fee investment value**

	ratio		
10	$172,790.24	$9,330.05	$163,460.19
20	$413,524.96	$42,134.52	$371,390.44
30	$805,656.46	$122,010.30	$683,646.16
40	$1,444,397.35	$291,826.44	$1,152,570.91

If you look carefully, you will notice how much a seemingly small amount of .85% can take out of the potential growth. If this young person started at 18, then at 58 years old, there would be almost $300,000 that is lost to fees! This is why fees and expenses are absolutely critical to pay attention to before investing in Mutual Funds or any fund for that matter.

Beyond expense ratios, finance websites will also show what is exactly in the portfolio. Meaning it will show all the different investments in the fund (also called **asset allocation**). The percentage and amount of each stock held, the type of investments, and the sectors. You can even get scores on whether the fund is good for the environment.

morningstar.com is one of the more popular sites to access this information.

Fund Types & Diversification

There are different types of fund strategies. Here are just some of them.

Equity refers to stock investments. But within this category there are different strategies. You could choose an Equity fund with an aggressive strategy (more risk) or an income strategy (dividends) or a value strategy (long term). The basic concept is to make the fund accomplish a certain goal based on the types of stocks invested.

Fixed-Income would invest in conservative and safe investments. The goal is to preserve income by investing in low risk, low return investments. This could include certain bonds or cash.

Index is tracking a list or index of stocks. For instance, the S&P 500 is an index of the 500 biggest companies in the United States. This fund invests proportionally in all 500 of those companies. (More on index funds later).

Balanced is what it sounds like. A mix of different investments in order to diversify.

International/Global invests in international stock and investments and may vary on the strategy.

WTF are ETFs?

ETF's are "exchange traded funds." The simple definition is that they are a "basket" of different stocks which are bundled and sold. They have some similarities to Mutual Funds and also have specific strategies and objectives, but one big difference is that ETF's are bought and sold on the market *throughout* the day as opposed to being priced at the end of the market day.

Here is how they work on a basic level. To give an example, let's say you want to do Halloween differently this year. Normally you buy an assortment of candy in a big bag, dump it in a bowl and kids come to trick or treat and you let them pick a few pieces. It is ok, but the selections in the bag are limited and the size might be too small and the kids in the neighborhood know you suck.

But what if you gave out mini baskets or bags of the very best candy? So, you decide to buy a box of all your favorites. You now have 15 boxes of candy.

Next, you take one piece or bar from each box and place it into one mini basket or bag. When kids come trick or treating you hand out a whole mini basket which contains 15 pieces of the very best candy. Halloween saved and kids willingly come to rake your yard and wash your car.

But you may also want to get really specific and group all the best chocolate candy in one bag and all the sour candy in another bag and lollipops in another bag. Then kids can have a choice based on what they like. Now you are acting and thinking like a fund manager!

ETF's have a similar journey. To simplify the process here is how they work on a basic level. There are fund managers or creators that come up with a strategy of what equities (for our purposes, stocks) to bundle. This all depends on the objective of the fund. The fund's goal may be to invest in a certain sector or it may be for diversification, or for growth, etc. Just like Mutual Funds.

For instance, there is an ETF fund called NERD which invests in e-gaming stocks/companies. So you could go out and buy those stocks individually OR you buy a share of the NERD ETF which gives you a strategic and proportional exposure based on the objectives and companies in the portfolio.

Once the fund concept is created, an **Authorized Participant** or

AP (which is a fancy name for an investment bank) will buy all the individual stocks for the fund manager or creator to bundle together. Think back to our candy analogy. This time you want to sell your bags. So you have an idea for some candy bags, so you ask your parents (APs) to buy all the boxes of candy, you bundle pieces together and then give the bags back to your parents to sell. You make a little percentage for managing and putting the fund together, your parents make money by selling the new basket or bag. There are few other nuances, but this is the gist.

The benefits of ETF's are they can be bought and sold throughout the day (unlike Mutual Funds). They do have expense ratios as well and so you should keep an eye on that because we saw how they make an impact on your investment. In general ETF's tend to be less in expenses than Mutual Funds, but not always.

Here are some unique and niche ETFs:

NERD – Video games/E-Sports
ROBO & BOTZ - AI / Machine Learning technology
HACK - Cyber security
SOCL - Social Networking
XAR - Aerospace & Defense
MJ - Marijuana industry
FIW – Water
XLC – Communications
SLIM – For FAT People
SDY – Dividend ETF

Again, you can always look up what is actually in the ETF just like a Mutual Fund.

MORE ABOUT INDEX FUNDS

In elementary school you learned the different parts of a book. You learned about the table of contents, some books had a glossary and an index. The index is a list of the content in the book. In the stock world, an index is also a list of stocks. There are different "books" though. The **Dow Jones** is a list of the 30 biggest stocks across sectors in the US. The **S&P 500** is a list of the 500 biggest companies in the US. The NASDAQ is a list of all the stocks listed on the NASDAQ stock exchange.

As they stand, they are just a list. They are also helpful tools to gauge how well the market is doing. This is why you will often hear that "the Dow Jones was up by 2 points today." This doesn't mean the entire stock market was up by two percent, only that particular index of 30 stocks collectively for better or for worse added up to a gain of two percent (also referred to as points).

But what if I didn't want to cherry pick or buy all 30 of those stocks or all 500 of the S&P stocks but wanted exposure to that entire list or index? You can!

An **Index Fund** does just that. But it is not its own thing like a Mutual Fund or ETF but is a type of fund investment. In other words, I am investing in a Mutual Fund or ETF which is "tracking" or more accurately investing in an index or list.

These are incredibly popular because they are typically very low in expenses because there isn't a lot of management required. It is simply investing in the list of stocks in proportion to their value. Index Funds are also popular because they have a standard of performance over time.

Quick tangent: on the topic of low-cost investing, with the advent of apps, robo investors, and online brokerages and even the popularity of low-cost investing brokerages like Vanguard, there is more competition and incentives to get investors to invest using their platform. One shift was the reduction of commissions on trades. For a long time, there would be a flat commission on trades (anywhere from $5-$10 per trade) but most brokerages have eliminated this fee. It is a great time to be alive, and this reduced barrier to entry has made investing more popular and even helped to facilitate the GameStop market event of 2021.

BUYING SHARES AND TIMING (Stop, Market, Limit)

When it comes time to buy or sell shares (stocks or funds), you may select the timing of when to make the transaction. If you use an online brokerage, you will find there are options in how or when to execute the trade.

To help us conceptualize this, let's think about concert tickets. You want to go see Travis Scott perform in 3 months and tickets for the concert are sold out. So, you go to your friend who is a ticket broker and he says ticket prices for that concert are now $200. If you buy them right now, you are buying them at the "market" price or the current price.

On the other hand, if you were trying to sell those tickets for $200 each and someone buys them, you *sold* them at "market" price or your current price.

In either case, you are buying or selling at the current or **market** price. Easy enough.

Now let's say there is a rumor Travis Scott will add another show. You can only go on the original date and $200 is still too expensive for you, but your budget would allow you to buy at $175. You ask your ticket broker friend, "hey, whether he adds another show or not, if the price falls to $175, buy it!" You just set a **limit** or specific price on when to buy the ticket.

Conversely if you are trying to sell, you tell your ticket broker friend, "if the demand or market for tickets hits $250, sell mine!" You set a limit or specific price on when to sell.

In both of these situations you are setting a **LIMIT** on when to buy or sell. It is a specific price you have in mind.

In our final scenario, tickets are $200 and you aren't sure if there is another concert being added. You tell your ticket broker friend "if the price for tickets goes up to $225, then buy!" The idea here is that while the price is not what you hoped for, you at least got the tickets before the price skyrocketed even higher. This number of $225 is telling your friend to **STOP** and buy at market price, right now. Your friend may not be able to get exactly $225 because the time your friend is alerted to the price it may have gone up a little. But this would be preferable than being forced to buy at say $500 or even more.

If you are selling, the same thing. Travis Scott announces another show and so you have already told your friend, if the price falls to $180, sell! The idea is to sell before the price drops too far where perhaps you lose money when you sell the tickets. You may not get exactly $180, but this amount tells your friend to STOP and sell at the market price.

In summary:

Market means buy or sell at the current price.

Limit means buy or sell at a specific price.

Stop means to buy or sell after a certain price is reached.

With that concert ticket example, let's apply it to buying and selling shares.

MARKET - If you desire to buy SNAP stock and simply want it right now and you aren't concerned about price, you select "market." Market means you are buying at the market price. The only downside would be if you want to buy a share at the market or current price of $50, you may not get the $50 price you saw listed but you will get the current price when the order is filled. This kind of extreme movement is not common, but could happen depending on the volatility of the stock or market. If you place an order after the market closes, the price will most likely be different when the market opens.

LIMIT (BUY) OR "BUY LIMIT" ORDER - A limit order is saying this is the highest or lowest amount you are willing to pay for a share. If you want to buy SNAP, but your limit is $50 a share, then the limit order option means it will fill your order at that specific price. Limits are not always guaranteed to execute or fill but are certainly a better option to get the price you want.

There is also an extra question asked on these asking how long to leave this order open. One option is ***Good until Canceled***, which means your order remains open until you cancel it. The other option is for ***Day Only*** which means it will only stay open for the trading day—if it doesn't fill, you can set it up again the next day if you so choose.

LIMIT (SELL) OR "SELL LIMIT" ORDER - This is the highest or lowest amount you are willing to sell a share. Let's say you want to sell the share when it reaches $42. Place a *sell limit order* with a price of $42. If the stock hits $42 or higher, the limit order would be triggered and the order is executed at $42 or above. Obviously if the share price does not hit $42 then it would not sell or execute.

STOP OR STOP LOSS - This option buys or sells shares once the predetermined price has been reached. Once the price is reached, it basically becomes a market order. If FATT stock is listed at $12 a share and you place a ***buy stop order*** for FATT stock at $10; once the share price hits $10, you will buy FATT at the market price. It may or may not be exactly $10 because the market may move more when the stop is triggered.

Same goes for selling. Let's say you want to sell FATT which is currently at $10 but when it hits $15. The Sell Stop order would sell at the market price once the share price hits $15.

STOP LIMIT - This option is just like a Stop or Stop loss except instead of triggering a market order, you trigger a limit. This is preferable to a market action because the order will execute closer to your desired price. As always, never a guarantee but certainly the better option.

You may also trigger stops by **trailing**. A **Trailing Stop Loss** can be by dollar amount or percent. This triggers a market action when the share price moves a certain amount up or down either by dollar amount or by percentage.

In general, if you can use limit orders this is the best option.

Dollar Cost Averaging

When you buy stock and you see green (or in the positive) you are feeling like a finance whiz. I mean stocks only go up, right? When it turns red or goes down, you start to panic. Did I buy too high? Do I cut my losses and get out? Is the market crashing? "If the forms of this world die, which is more real, the me that dies or the me that's infinite?[9]"

Well, a strategy that some investors use to calm down is called **dollar cost averaging**. To illustrate, let's compare two stocks and assume you have $100 to invest each month.

The first stock we will call the King Hippo Corporation or KHPO

In the first month you have $100 to invest and KHPO is at $10/share. So you buy 10 shares (10x10=100).

In the second month, you have another $100 to invest. KHPO is now at $12. Good pick! So you buy another $100 worth or 8.33 shares. (100/12 = 8.33). Now you have 18.33 shares.

Month 3, KHPO is up to $15! You buy $100 shares worth of stock again or 6 ⅔ shares. (100/15=6.66)

After 3 months, you invested $300 and now own 25 shares! Worth $375 ($15 x 25 shares). So you have a net of $75 ($375 - $300 invested). See chart below.

---

[9] Albert Markovski in I Heart Huckabees (film), 2004

	Month 1	**Month 2**	**Month 3**
Share Price	$10	$12	$15
Shares Bought	10 Shares	10 + 8.33 = 18.33 Shares	18.33 + 6.66 = 25 Shares
Total Value	$100	$219.96	$375

Now let's try a different stock. We will call it Soda Popinski Inc. or SPOP

In the first month you invest $100 and it also starts at $10. So you have 10 shares of SPOP

But in month 2, SPOP drops significantly. It drops to $1 a share! Now, you can cut your losses but let's say you are confident in the company because you use their products. You know this is temporary. So, you "buy the dip" which is a term to describe buying shares when they are down from a higher price point. You buy $100 worth. So now you have 110 shares! It is worth $110 (110 shares at $1).

Month 3, as you believed would happen, SPOP goes up again. Nowhere near $10 but goes to $5. You buy another $100 worth or 20 shares. You now have 130 shares of SPOP at $5. It is half the price from its high two months ago, but you have more shares. Your 130 shares x $5 is worth $650. You spent $300 so your net is $350. See chart for the action.

	Month 1	Month 2	Month 3
Share Price	$10	$1	$5
Shares Bought	10 Shares	10 + 100 = 110 Shares	110 + 20 = 130 Shares
Total Value	$100	$110	$650

KHPO which only went up and up and up gave you **$75 net**

SPOP which went down a lot and up a little gave you **$350 net**

The idea behind Dollar Cost Averaging is to invest at regular intervals even if the stock price goes down because you are buying more and more shares. And when the price goes up, it impacts <u>all the shares</u> you own.

This strategy can be helpful to stick to your plan and not let emotions get the best of you. Take it for what it is, a sound strategy. It is not a guarantee.

Cost Basis and Capital Gains

Before you get too excited about *stonks*, Uncle Sam is not the fun uncle you thought he is, but is here to kill your buzz. Income you make from your amazing stock trading skills are taxable.

This is called a **capital gains tax**. This tax is calculated on what is called your **cost basis**. This is essentially the positive difference between the sale price of an asset and its original purchase price. Example: You bought POO stock at $20 a share (your cost basis) and sold it at $25 a share, so you are taxed on $5.

Note that the word is asset. Your Pokémon collection or jewelry or real estate or game show winnings are included as assets. Of course, if you lost money in the stock market you can help off-set your tax burden by deducting **capital losses** that occur when an asset is sold for less than the original purchase price. If you bought POO for $20 and sold for $15, you have a capital loss of $5.

These taxes are only realized when you sell. If your account is up $1000 you aren't taxed on any of that until you sell. If this money is in a tax-advantaged account (like a retirement account, explained later) then you do not get hit with capital gains.

There are two types of capital gains tax: short-term and long-term.

Short-term capital gains tax are the profits you make from the sale of an asset held for one year or less. These gains are taxed at income tax rates and will be added to your adjusted gross income. Meaning, if you make $35,000 a year your tax rate is 12%, but if you sold stock and made $10,000 in gains and only held the shares for less than a year, your new taxable amount is $45,000 and you are now in the 22% federal tax rate.

Long-term capital gains tax are the profits from the sale of an asset held for more than a year.

In general, this is much more tax friendly. The income is also not included in your annual income unlike the short-term gains.

Below is a chart for long-term capital gains taxes on an individual filer (again if you have a tax status of joint or head of household, it looks different.)

Long-term capital gains tax rate	**The Net Income**
0%	$0 to $40,000
15%	$40,001 to $441,450
20%	$441,451 or more

Oh and don't forget, States also get their piece of your investment prowess. Be sure to look up your state. Some states do not (Alaska, Florida, New Hampshire, Nevada, South Dakota, Tennessee, Texas, Washington, Wyoming) but all the other states do. And some great states like California don't care if it's short or long, you get taxed at income tax levels no matter what, which is a bummer.

OPTION CONTRACTS

Warning! Warning! This is advanced investing. With the ease of investing with apps it is important to know what option contracts are since they are readily available on stock trading apps.

On a very basic level, an **option** is a contract which gives you the right but not the obligation to a future action. Simplified even further, you are paying a non-refundable amount of money in exchange for the option to an action at a later date.

That's the technical definition, but let's try to understand the concept using the example of airline flights. Let's assume you are planning a flight to Dalla's to meet a friend who lives on the other side of the country. You aren't 100% sure if your friend will be able to meet you, but plane ticket prices are really good right now. They are only $199 round trip. In our magical world let's assume you actually could buy a non-refundable contract for $9 which would give you the *option* to buy that plane ticket at a later date within the next 2 months for the price it is right now or $199.

This would be a really nice option to have because if the price of the ticket goes up to $300 as plane tickets often do, and your friend finally confirms the meet up, you may buy the ticket at $199 even though the current price is $300. All you paid was $9 extra dollars for that option. All in all, to secure that price and take the flight you paid $208. A savings of $92.

Conversely, if the ticket price drops to $119 for some reason or your friend cannot go, you let the contract expire. You paid $9, but remember it is the right but not the obligation to buy. In essence, you were able to lock in a low price for a later purchase or get "insurance" if you couldn't go.

In this airline ticket case, you are betting the price of your plane ticket is going up. This is a **call** or "going long." A way to remember what a call is to think of the expression (especially if you grew up with siblings) "I call shotgun" meaning you want the front seat and "call" it early. One goal of a call is to buy early or buy low and at some point sell high.

Back to stocks. Let's say you believe WIZZ stock is going to go up and it's currently priced at $44 a share. You would check out something called an **options chain**. The options chain is a chart showing how much a contract costs based on the **strike price**.

The strike price is the market price of the stock that you must beat in order for you to be "in the money."

To give another example let's use gambling on a football game. Let's say the Raiders are 3 point favorites to win over the Jaguars. This means in order for you to be "in the money" or win, you would need to bet on the Raiders and hope they win by at least 4 (the strike) against the Jaguars.

Back to the options chain, you will see a chart of different strike prices and the cost of the contract. The price is listed for s ingle share, but the contract is sold in packages of 100. Hence, be sure to multiply that price by 100 to get a more accurate contract price. The contract price is based off of a formula, consult a finance or math major if you are interested in learning more. In short, it calculates the aspects making up the contract such as time, the inherent value, volatility, etc.

To keep it simple, here is a basic options chain chart:

STOCK: WIZZ
EXPIRATION: 12/31/2020 (30 Days)
CALLS__________| |PUTS__________

BID	ASK	STRIKE	BID	ASK
3.30	3.65	43.00	1.87	2.13
3.00	3.40	43.50	2.13	2.36
2.82	3.15	44.00	2.37	2.63
2.68	2.84	44.50	2.66	2.89

2.40	2.57	45.00	2.92	3.15
2.16	2.40	45.50	3.20	3.45

Let's assume the current price of WIZZ is $44.00. If you believe WIZZ is going to go above $46 in the next month, you could buy a CALL contract.

You decide to buy a contract at the strike price of 45.50. This means you want to be able to have the option to buy WIZZ stock at 45.50. You have this feeling that WIZZ will go up to $55 in the next month. Looking at the chart, you find the Strike Price of 45.50 and you will see on the Call side (left side) two categories: bid and ask.

To reset an earlier discussion on buying stock, BID is how much someone is willing to pay and ASK is what the seller is willing to sell. Per our previous discussion, if you place a Market Order you will receive the ask price or 2.40. If you really want that 2.16 you could place a limit order, but also know that there are no guarantees it will fill. If you are able to avoid market orders, then do. Let's say you place a limit at 2.25 and it fills! You have paid $2.25 per share for the option to buy at $45.50 per share within the next month (before expiration) as long as it beats the strike price. Again, while contracts are priced in single units, they are sold in packages of 100. This means you aren't buying an option on 1 share but 100 shares. Your contract price is now 2.25 x 100 or $225. This money is gone no matter what happens. To see how you might fare, look at this chart:

Share Price at Expiration	Total Value of Shares (x100)	Cost to purchase shares ($4550) + contract ($225)	Net Gain/Loss
45.50	4550	4775	-225
46	4600	4775	-175
46.50	4650	4775	-125
47.00	4700	4775	-75
47.75	4775	4775	0
50	5000	4775	+225
55	5500	4775	+725

With the contract price, the only way to make money is if the share price hits $48 or higher. Even though the strike price is $45.50, you wouldn't exercise this option unless the share price hit above $48. But beware! Check with your broker or brokerage. Typically, your default position is to exercise the option if the strike price is met at expiration.

But what if I don't intend on really buying all that stock? Well, you can also sell just the contract because it has value. You wouldn't get paid the underlying value of stocks, only the value of the contract. If the contract is priced at $3.10 and there are 100 shares in a contract, the contract price is $310. The contract may gain or lose value as it approaches expiration.

To give an example let us assume you bought a $15 call for RAD and it expires in 2 weeks. The price of RAD when you bought the call was $14.50

The contract price was $1.00 so you paid $100. In order for you to make money the stock price would need to get beyond $16 (strike price + cost of contract). Today, the stock price hits $14.90 and the option contract goes up in value to $1.10. You could sell that option. In which case you paid $100, but sold it for $110. You made profit without hitting the strike.

You as an investor could also "write contracts." This means you collect that premium or contract price. You can write **naked calls** for instance, in which case you are responsible for buying the shares should the person on the other side of the contract exercise their option. This could be very dangerous as the share price technically has no limit. You could be on the hook for buying shares at prices you cannot afford. **Covered calls** are where you write the contract but you actually have the shares in your possession. If the other person exercises their option, you have the shares already and can deliver them without concern about the share price.

PUTS

Puts are the other side of the option. You believe a stock is going down. If our same stock, WIZZ is at 44.00 and you believe it will plummet to $35, then you could buy a put. This gives you the right but not the obligation to sell at a fixed price. Look at the puts side or right side of the chart:

STOCK: WIZZ
EXPIRATION: 12/31/2020 (30 Days)
CALLS____________| |PUTS____________

BID	ASK	STRIKE	BID	ASK
3.30	3.65	43.00	1.87	2.13
3.00	3.40	43.50	2.13	2.36
2.82	3.15	44.00	2.37	2.63
2.68	2.84	44.50	2.66	2.89
2.40	2.57	45.00	2.92	3.15
2.16	2.40	45.50	3.20	3.45

You decide to buy a put contract with a strike price of 43.00. Once again, the bid is what people are willing to pay and ask is what people are willing to sell. If you buy a market order, it will be 2.13. Again, you choose a limit order this time of an even 2.00

Share Price at Expiration	Total Value of Shares (x100)	Cost to purchase shares + contract ($200)	Sold at 43.00 Net Gain/Loss
35	3500	3700	+600
40	4000	4200	+100
41	4100	4300	0

42	4200	4400	-100
43	4300	4500	-200

As you can see from the chart, the stock would need to drop from 44 to below 41 in order for you to make money in this scenario. Again, contract prices may vary and the amount of movement the stock needs to make in order for you to make money will also vary.

The examples above were to give you a basic sense of how options work. There are other strategies such as a **Bull Put Spread** you can utilize. But if you really want to learn options, open up a practice account with imaginary money first and learn. The options world is filled with professionals. Would you play against a poker champion in poker with your own money? This is effectively what you are doing when you mess with options. If you learn them and understand them they can be a great hedge and diversification strategy, but education is absolutely necessary.

SHORT SELLING

Another clever feature in your brokerage account is the ability to trade on margin. This is another way of saying you can borrow shares to sell with the expectation you will return the shares later. More on that in a minute. But selling short or shorting means your objective is to borrow shares, sell them now and rebuy at a lower price.

To give a different example. Let's say you are house sitting for a family. They are gone for 2 months over Thanksgiving and Christmas Break and plan to do their gift exchanges in late January. As you make yourself at home you notice a brand new unopened PS5 in the garage. You also know PS5's are selling for a premium (about $1,000) during Christmas. You decide to "borrow" the PS5 and sell it right now for $1,000. About a week before the family returns you will go buy another one at $750 because the price should drop after Christmas and as supply ramps up. In this case you made $250 without spending any of your money. Obviously, there is a huge risk. What if the price doesn't drop but goes up? Or cannot get a PS5. You bear that expense and consequence.

Back to shorting stock. You believe the stock SUCK is going to drop. It is listed at $80 a share. You borrow 100 shares of SUCK from your brokerage. This would be $8,000 (80 x 100). But you should know that the brokerage would require 50% of your own money in the margin account and you would borrow the other 50% with interest! So, you are borrowing $4,000 and being charged interest on it. Usually you may keep your short position open as long as you'd like. Keeping in mind you are being charged interest on what you borrowed.

Here is a glance at what could happen:

You short 100 shares of SUCK @ $80 = $8,000

Stock price drops to $69, you buy back 100 shares of SUCK @ $69, total cost $6,900

Total profit = $8,000 - $6,900 = $1100

You won that round!

Now, let's say you short 100 shares of SUCK @ $80 = $8,000

Stock price increases and remains at $100

To stop the bleeding, you buy back 100 shares of SUCK at $100: total cost = $10,000

Total loss: $8,000 - $10,000 = - $2000

NOTE: The maximum loss on a short is unlimited as the stock price could theoretically increase forever. The drama of the GameStop short in 2021 is an example.

Again, there are more layers involved as there are some shares which are labeled as "easy to borrow" and "hard to borrow." This can change not only the margin interest but may also require the shares you borrow to be called back without your say so. These details are beyond an introduction, but again this is very much an advanced move even though brokerages make it easy to participate and "FinTok" videos make it sound easy. GameStop anyone?

BONDS

Shifting gears to something less risky. We discussed earlier how making debt payments is painful and ideally a position we are never in. But, what if we can be on the other side and make money off of debt payments? This is basically a bond.

When a company wants to raise money they can issue shares, but what if a company doesn't want to issue secondary shares? Is there another way to raise money? Yes, through bonds.

Bonds are debt instruments (and also considered an "equity" because you "own" their debt). To simplify, just think about someone who wants to borrow money from you. You have some basic questions: how much do they want to borrow, and when will they pay me back? Another question in the back of your mind is what is the likelihood they will pay you back. Let's be honest, some of us have that one friend where we know if we lend out money, we will never see it again.

A quick life tangent: If you are the type of person who knows to the penny what someone owes you and constantly reminds them and constantly worries about getting paid back, you may want to examine that side of you. It is certainly good you are on top of your finances and good that you follow up. But always keeping score and doing constant bookkeeping is no way to live either. You will be miserable. This will consume your thinking and you will become more and more of a calculator and less of a human being. You can lose respect from friends if you only view them in terms of who owes you what and constantly reminding them of that fact. The time spent with your friends is more important than getting your $15 back by the end of the night. When you are on your deathbed you won't even remember what you did with the $15, but you will remember your friendships. You don't want to come across as someone who cares more about your bank account than being in the presence of other people. Practicing generosity regularly helps to correct a scorekeeping mindset. Tangent over.

Back to Bonds. So, you lend out money to a friend, but let's say it is a much bigger amount of money. At that point, that money you lend is lost interest you could be making, plus there is a risk associated with lending money out. What if I don't get it back? As we talked about earlier, interest is essentially the cost of borrowing money.

To make it worth your while to loan out the money and to incentivize your friend to pay it back, you loan out $5000 at 5% interest (annually). This means that your friend will pay you back

$5,250 at the end of the year.

Outside of friends, bonds are also issued by companies or governments (local, state or federal) as a way to bring in revenue or fund projects. Let's start with corporate or company bonds. Let's say Apple, Inc. issues bonds and you are interested in buying one for diversification purposes.

The typical structure would look like this: You buy 1 bond with a "face value" of $1,000. So, you would give Apple $1,000 for the bond. The face value means when you redeem the bond, you get the **face value** also known as **par value** which is $1,000.

The length of time your money is being borrowed varies from bond to bond. You want to look for the **maturity date.** This is when the bond may be redeemed for that face value amount.

The Apple bond in our example "matures" in 3 years from today and the "**coupon rate**" or interest is 5%.

Quick history lesson: the reason the interest payments are called **coupons** is because original bonds actually had physical coupons attached to them you would redeem for the interest payment. Everything is done electronically now, so they are not needed anymore but the name stuck.

Here is what all this means. You give Apple $1,000 of your hard-earned money. In exchange they issue you a bond which says that in 3 years we will pay you back the full face value of that bond (or $1,000) *AND* we will also pay you 5% on that amount every 6 months until it matures, or the three years is up.

The math looks like this: To start, you are -$1,000 because you gave it to Apple to borrow.

Year 1, Coupon 1 - you get paid $50 (5% of 1,000)

Year 1, Coupon 2 - you get paid another $50

Year 2, Coupon 1 - you get paid $50

Year 2, Coupon 2 - you get paid $50

Year 3, Coupon 1 - you get $50

Year 3, Coupon 2 - you get $50

End of year 3, the bond "matures" and you get paid back your $1,000.

In 3 years you gave Apple $1,000 but you received $1300 at the end of three years for a net of **$300**.

The way investors calculate the value of the bond is by its **yield**. In this case the yield is 5%. This is calculated by taking the coupon payment ($50) and dividing it by the face value ($1000). 50/1000 = 5%

But what if I want to sell my bond before the three years? Let's say I need that money back. Can I cash it in early? No you cannot, but what you can do is sell it to another investor!

This means someone else will get the coupon payments *and* the face value or par value of the bond when it matures. You get your cash today and they get the remaining benefits of the bond.

Here is the thing though. Because bonds are tied to interest rates, their value and yield can change. You may not be able to sell your bond for the price you paid for it.

Here is an example. Let's say you want to sell your Apple 3-year bond after only 1 year of holding it. There are 2 more years of coupon payments left ($200) and the face value of the bond ($1,000).

Johnny Investor wants to buy an Apple bond but the one you have is not as good as the new Apple bonds being issued. Apple issues another bond today, but instead of 5% it is now 7%!

Why would Johnny want to buy a bond like yours with 5% interest when he can pay the same amount and get 7%! This is why your bond price will go down. If you hold onto it, it doesn't matter; but if you want to sell it, your bond price goes down.

Why? Johnny will not pay for your bond when he can get something that makes more money for the same price. You would have to lower the price of your bond to make it more appealing. This is called a **discount**. What does this mean? In order for you to match the yield of the 7% bond, you would have to sell yours for $963 dollars instead of $1,000.

Here is the math. The better bond that pays 7% ($70 coupon payment) x 6 times (before maturity) = $420 (nice) + $1,000 (face value) = $1,420.

In this case, Johnny spent $1,000 to make $420. The yield to maturity is 7%.

Your bond on the other hand, has 2 years left with 5% interest so $50 x 4 times (4 remaining coupon payments) = $200 + $1,000 (face) = $1,200

To match the better bond, you sold yours at $963 for Johnny to make $200. This also is a yield to maturity of 7%. The amounts might be different, but the return is 7% in both cases.

The specific equations for bonds and bond yields are beyond our scope, but there are plenty of bond calculators on the internet. The point is to show that if the interest goes up, the bond price falls. This is because your bond is not as lucrative or desirable.

However, if interest falls your bond price rises. This means you could sell your bond for more than the face. Someone would gladly pay you more for a bond that yields more interest than a low interest bond. This is called a **premium.**

Premium = pay more for

Discount = pay less for

Here are a few other aspects you need to consider before purchasing a bond.

Callable or Non-Callable bonds. All this means is that a company can "call back" a callable bond before the maturity date. If you were planning on 5 years of interest payments, but the bond you have is **callable** and they call it back, even if there are 3 years left, you get your face value back, but lose out on those 3 years of interest!

Non-callable of course means the company can't and won't call it back. This means the coupon or interest payments will be made until the maturity date.

Zero Coupons. There are bonds which do not offer any coupons or interest payments. Wait, so why would I buy it? Because these bonds are sold at a **discount**. This means that a zero-coupon bond with a face of $1,000 might sell for $800.

At the end of 3 years you originally paid $800 and got $1000. Even without interest payments, you are still making money.

This is a nice segue into government bonds or Treasuries.

TREASURIES

Treasuries are effectively government bonds. The Treasury Department issues four main types of these securities.

Treasury bills (or T-bills) - these "bonds" mature in one year or less. These are considered incredibly safe and many investors and governments around the world invest in these for safety. There are no interest or coupon payments, but they are sold at a slight **discount** of their face value. To give an example, let's say the Treasury issued a 52-week T-bill at $97 for a $100 face value T-bill. This means you pay $97 dollars today and in 1 year, you will receive the face value of $100. The Treasury Department auctions new T-bills throughout the year and the discount rate changes often.

Treasury notes (or T-notes) - these "bonds" take a little bit longer to mature. The maturity lengths are between two and ten years. These are structured more like the typical bonds discussed earlier. **T-notes** issue interest or "coupon" payments every six months, but the "coupon rate" is based on one year. For example, a $10,000 10-year treasury note with a coupon rate of 2.00% means every six months, you'll receive a payment of $100.00. If you add up the two coupon payments for the year it equals to 2% of the face value ($200). At maturity, you would redeem it for the full $10,000.

It is also worth noting that the 10-year treasury note is a popular benchmark for measuring economic sentiment. If investors are uncertain, these are popular safe havens. If investors are confident, then they will risk elsewhere because there are better returns to be found. And while mortgage rates (home loans) are not directly connected to 10-year Treasury notes, the 10-year note has substantial influence on current mortgage rates (more on mortgages later).

Treasury bonds (or T-bonds) - the only difference between these and T-notes are length of maturity. These have maturity dates of ten years to thirty years in the United States. Some countries have tried to issue 100-year bonds! They have a coupon payment every six months and are redeemed at their face value upon maturity.

Savings bonds - These used to be popular gifts from grandparents to their grandkids. These are zero-coupon bonds and sold at a discount. However, there is interest that will be paid out when the bond is redeemed or it matures. The interest is low but it does compound. On a 30 years savings bond, the bond ceases to generate interest.

For example, a 30-year Savings Bond issued in December 1992 with a face of $100 and a 4% interest rate cost $50 to purchase. After 28 years it is now valued at $191.56. With $141.56 interest accumulated so far. Once December 2022 arrives, there will be no more interest, but the amount at redemption should be a little over $200. Not a bad return on $50, although it took a long time!

Municipal Bonds - These bonds are also government issued, but not from the Treasury. These are bonds issued by state and local governments. They do however carry a tax advantage. Depending on where you live and the municipality (local government) issuing the bonds you could earn interest on these bonds tax-free. These are nice if you are older and trying to preserve income.

Why would I get bonds?

These are considered a healthy part of a portfolio due to their relative safety, steady income, and can be a nice way to diversify. While not always the case, bonds have historically done better when the stock market is struggling, hence the diversification strategy.

Bond Funds

Remember ETF's and Mutual Funds? Well, you can get exposure to bonds through these funds too! They can range from high yield (risky) bond funds, to safer Treasury bonds funds. Some examples are listed in the next section on investment strategies.

INVESTMENT STRATEGIES

…And here we are. There are different strategies on how to invest. It is up to you to do your own research or talk to a wealth management professional, but here are a few strategies to research or to get the mind going.

60/40

One is to do a mix of bonds and stocks at 60/40. This means 60% of your investment is in stocks and 40% in bonds.

This could be as simple as 60% in the S&P 500 Index (SPY or VOO)

And 40% in a Bond Fund (VBTLX or FTBFX)

Some believe this is sure and steady, others argue there is too much weight on bonds. If you are younger, there is a good reason to consider taking on more risk (more stock).

Low Cost

An example for a 20-year-old with $10,000 to invest might look like this:

$4800 in VTI or SCHB (this is the total US Stock Market). Amount calculated by taking 60 (percent)/10,000 (total amount to invest) =.006 x (100 - your age (20); or 80) = $4800

$3200 in VTIAX or SWISX (this is total international stocks) Amount calculated by taking 40 (percent)/10,000 (total amount to invest) =.006 x (100 - your age (20); or 80) = $3200

$2000 in VSIGX or SCHR (these are Intermediate Bond Treasuries) Amount calculated by taking $10,000 x (your current age in %; or .20) = $2000

Target Date

A Target Date Fund is managed with diversification built-in. For a 25-year-old it would look similar to the portfolio above except it would weigh much heavier on stocks while young and slowly rebalance as you get older and closer to retirement. Check out FDKVX or VTTSX for an example of a 2060 Target Date Fund.

"All Seasons" and "Dragon" Portfolio

There are some newer suggestions for portfolios and the ratio amounts vary slightly, but the idea is to add more diversification with commodities, gold, and option contracts to account for volatility. An analysis is beyond our scope, but consider the ratio below.

30% Total Stock Market

40% Long Term Bonds

15% Intermediate Bonds (treasury bonds)

7.5% Commodities (oil, wheat, etc.)

7.5% Gold

A QUICK NOTE ABOUT OTHER INVESTMENTS

If you have established a firm foundation of personal finance and have an understanding then you can look into other types of investments to diversify even further. Some areas to research are cryptocurrency, FOREX, precious metals and even commodities. It is beyond the scope of this book to go into each but here is a very brief glossary:

Precious Metals: Gold, Silver, etc. can be bought and invested in directly or through ETF's and Mutual Funds. Metals are seen as a safe haven investment especially in times of recession because they are physical commodities with practical uses. They are also in limited supply (can't make more, you can only mine) which also gives them value.

Cryptocurrency: These are digital currencies you've certainly heard of like Bitcoin, Ethereum, etc. Cryptocurrency has been described as like digital gold. There is a finite amount, cannot be duplicated or printed, and is peer-to-peer meaning transactions are decentralized from a bank or processing company. This is still a relatively young asset so do your research and using our earlier principle, think of it in terms of a potential diversified investment as opposed to a sole investment vehicle.

FOREX: You may have seen dudes on Instagram with sportscars advocating for FOREX. It stands for Foreign Exchange and it is simply betting that one currency (Euro, Pound, Yen, etc.) will rise or fall in value relative to another. The goal is to buy another currency low, wait for it to rise and sell high. You can also dabble in options (like stocks) on currency as well.

Commodities: With commodities you can also invest in everyday consumer goods like oil, or wheat or orange juice or bacon or coffee or beef and so on. The purpose is not to buy the physical goods, but to buy and sell contracts. The objective is to buy a commodity contract low and sell it high. But be careful, if you forget to close out contracts you may have to actually take delivery of the items. If you want exposure to commodities, stick to ETF's.

INSURANCE

The Gecko, the General, Jake, Flo, Mayhem you see them all the time. Why?

To begin, you may have seen unboxing videos where someone buys a brand new iPhone only to drop it and crack the screen on the first day. A very expensive purchase is ruined just like that. But what about things even more expensive than a new iPhone? For instance, cars, homes and your own health. While you may be able to fix your phone screen or buy a new one, you may not have the means to buy another car or a home or pay for an expensive medical procedure. This is where insurance comes in. The objective of insurance is to preserve your savings and keep you from going into massive debt.

The first type to learn about is **P&C Insurance** or "property and casualty" insurance.

The concept of insurance from the insurance company's perspective is like a Vegas casino. To explain: if you go to Vegas and play blackjack or play craps, there are odds attached to the likelihood of you winning. The Casino is in the business of winning and so the odds are set to be in favor of the House (Casino). This basically means if you are really good at gambling and you played 100 games, "the House" or the Casino would win at least 51 times. The odds vary from game to game and some games are better than others, but you get the idea.

You go to Vegas for a good time and try to win some money, and you may very well win and win big, but the odds are not in your favor. Insurance is structured similarly. What the insurance companies do is to promise to cover or insure up to a certain amount. They calculate the odds of you actually needing or claiming this money and they factor it into the price you pay.

Let's start with car insurance on a basic level and get into types of coverage later. There are some liabilities and risks every time you drive. To give a few examples, there is the risk that you wreck your own car. There is a risk you wreck someone else's car. There is a risk you hurt yourself and a risk you hurt someone else. And there is a risk you ruin someone else's property.

To indemnify or "make whole" or pay for the damage can be really really expensive. Especially if you wreck your car, another car, a person's house property, hurt the other driver and yourself!

The insurance company will insure or "protect" your expenses up to a certain amount. Again, the idea is to help preserve your savings.

They calculate the odds of you needing this money, the severity of accidents, etc. and they build it into the cost with two payments you are responsible for: the **premium** and the **deductible**.

The **premium** is the amount you pay to keep the policy or keep the insurance going. Think of a premium as a subscription. When you subscribe to Netflix it gives you access to watch shows on their platform. Likewise, with insurance, when you pay a premium, it gives you the right to "file a claim" should you need to fix/repair/replace something. Now, if you pay for Netflix but never watch a show, you still have to pay. Netflix gets paid whether you watch shows or not. Insurance premiums work the same way. In most cases, you will not get that premium money back. The premium allows you the opportunity to file a claim if there is a legitimate need to do so (more on that later).

The other expense is a **deductible**. The deductible is an amount of money you pay when you file a claim. For instance, your car insurance may allow for free towing services or help if your key is locked in your car. This is part of the basic insurance and included in paying your premium. But if you need to replace a fender or get body work repairs, this is not covered in the premium and so you need to pay the deductible.

The deductible is the amount of money you pay out of your own pocket <u>first</u> before the insurance company covers up to what they promise to insure you up to. Why? A few reasons. This helps keep you honest. You have "skin in the game." In other words, if you know you have to pay more money beyond the premium to fix something, there is a likelihood you will be a more cautious driver because it will cost you more if you are not. The other reason is financial. The deductible helps to offset the larger costs incurred by the insurance company. Remember, they are businesses. They exist to make money. They are publicly traded companies and people own shares in these companies. This is why a large percentage of commercials you see on TV are insurance related.

There is also an inverse relationship with premiums and deductibles. The more you pay in premiums, the less you will pay in deductibles. And the more you pay in deductibles, the less you pay in premiums. So, if you are accident prone, you are probably better off paying higher premiums. The insurance company will most likely make that adjustment. Again, they are doing the math and the odds based on all sorts of factors.

Back to the casino analogy: the sportsbooks in Vegas (the place that sets odds for sports betting) are typically fairly accurate on the point spread and total points and winners. How? They have a ton of data and information. So do insurance companies. For example, a 17-year-old boy with a 2.5 GPA with a sports car statistically has a way higher risk and expense than a 45-year-old woman lawyer driving a sedan. You might think, well that's common sense, but they also have the data to back it up. The data correlates to the risk, and the insurance company factors it in the price.

To summarize the whole process, you apply for coverage of something. You give all the information about what it is you are protecting and how much you want to protect. The insurance company gives a **quote** which includes a premium amount and a deductible amount. You pay the premium to keep the policy "in force" or active. If you file a claim, a claims adjuster (someone who examines the loss or damage and assesses a value) gives their findings to the insurance company and based on your policy limits and the claims adjuster's report, you can receive your reimbursement once you have satisfied or paid the deductible amount. It seems like a lot, but they walk you through it because, after all, you are paying for it.

On that note, let's talk further about car or auto insurance.

Car Insurance

Car insurance has many sides to it. A small fender bender may be common, but there can be damage done to property and life.

What happens if you get hit but the other person does not have insurance? We can get wild with situations, but here are the basic aspects of auto insurance. Each of these categories below carries a specific limit to it and as always, there may be a deductible attached to any claims you file. As you dissect and understand your policy, you can find out what is included, what isn't, and how much you are covered in each category.

Collision coverage pays for vehicle damage caused by crashes. If I rear-ended your car and damaged your bumper, collision coverage would help with this expense.

Comprehensive coverage pays for vehicle damage not caused by crashes. This may include incidents such as theft or if a tree falls on your car.

Liability coverage applies to injuries that you as the driver or policyholder cause to someone else. This is known as *bodily injury liability coverage.*

The other type of liability is *property damage liability coverage.* If you fell asleep at the wheel and crashed into a house, this would help cover the property damage.

Underinsured motorist coverage is intended for situations where you are hit by an uninsured driver or a driver who doesn't have enough insurance to pay for your total loss. This could also include if you are out for a walk or bike ride and get hit, and the driver flees. This coverage may or may not be required in your state. Which brings up the fact that there are other optional protections you can pick up such as **medical payments coverage**. If you are injured in a car accident, medical payments coverage may be able to help pay for expenses for medical treatment for you and any passengers.

While this is not true in every situation and every type of coverage, a good rule of thumb is to remember car insurance typically follows the car and <u>not</u> the driver. This point is being brought up to you to think twice before you let someone borrow *your* car. Their mistake hurts you.

One of the reasons you get an insurance agent is to walk through the coverage required for you and your family in order to make sure you are fully covered.

Home Insurance

With a thorough background in how insurance works and going through auto coverage, other types like home insurance are easy to understand. Home insurance covers damage and theft *on* and *done to* your property. It is important to know exactly what your policy will cover. For instance, damage caused by floods or earthquakes is not covered by home insurance. You would need to get separate policies to cover your home in case of damage incurred from natural disasters. Home insurance is also required in most cases if you are getting a home loan.

There are a couple options when it comes to insuring your property and this also applies to auto insurance as well. One is called **actual cash value** (ACV) and the other is called **replacement cost coverage**. A simplified example would be your 2018 MacBook got destroyed because a water heater broke and your computer was on the ground at the time and got soaked and your insurance decided to cover the loss. The actual cash value would be a reimbursement of what the value of a used 2018 MacBook is today. In other words, it accounts for depreciation and usage. You may have paid $1,999 for a MacBook but the actual cash value of a used 2018 MacBook is $1600. So, you got $1600 for a new computer or to buy a used one.

Replacement cost coverage on the other hand would allow you to get a new MacBook to replace the old one. You would pay more in premiums for this option. In either case, there is most likely a deductible required to satisfy first.

Keep documentation of items which are incredibly valuable and be specific. If you had a Chromebook but said you really had a MacBook Pro, this is insurance fraud and illegal. You would need to provide some sort of proof you owned a MacBook Pro. Photos and receipts are helpful with claims adjusters.

Renters Insurance

One of the nice parts of not owning a home is that you are not responsible for major damage. However, it is recommended to carry **renter's insurance** if you are renting. Typically, renter's insurance covers your personal property within the confines of the place you are renting. Again, there is the option of ACV and replacement cost. Renter's insurance is generally inexpensive to carry.

Life Insurance

In the hustle and bustle of life we often forget about our impact. If you haven't experienced the loss of a loved one, you certainly know someone who has. Beyond the grieving is also figuring out how to move on, but also the financial obligations of final costs and funerals as well as covering income especially if the deceased was a major provider in the family. **Life insurance** exists to provide relief. The basic premise is to buy a policy that will pay out a certain amount at your death to a **beneficiary**. A beneficiary means the person receiving the funds.

The life insurance policy remains in force by paying premiums (just like in car and home insurance). But because everyone will die, this changes the dynamic in how policies are obtained and paid for. In most cases, you will need to complete a very thorough medical history form and also have a medical exam. This information helps to determine if you are able to get covered and for how much. There are professionals known as **actuaries** which have enormous amounts of data, do calculations and essentially predict when and how you will die. (This is slight hyperbole, but not by much). The life insurance companies need to be able to make sure they can pay out the policy, cover their expenses and still make money. Obviously, it wouldn't make financial sense for an insurance company to offer a 1 Million dollar policy on someone who is 2 weeks away from dying, so their math and data helps guide their quotes and approvals.

There are different types of life insurance available, but here are some basic ones.

Term - Term is what it sounds like, coverage for a specified term. This insurance is typically for a 30-year period, but you can get 15 years, or 20 years etc. The premiums are the most economical. Like other forms of insurance, you do not get your premium back if you don't use it. The downside is if you outlive the term, you would need to reapply, or convert to a permanent policy. The premiums will be significantly higher the second time around, and there is a risk of not being covered. Overall, this is the most economical option. The amount recommended for coverage is 10 times your annual income.

Permanent or Whole - This insurance is a policy which covers you until you die, but also includes a cash value component. These policies may also be sold as IUL's (Indexed Universal Life policies) and VUL (Variable Universal Life policies). When you set up your policy, you are paying for a death benefit, but also putting money into a cash value account. These policies are expensive because you are paying for insurance and contributing cash into the policy. This policy is a little more complex than what it is typically sold or advertised as. The policy is fee heavy, and has a lot of rules and limitations. These may work for you, but for most, if you do the math, you are better off getting a Term Life policy and investing the rest somewhere else. It is recommended to get a second opinion from someone other than the person selling you this policy to see if this makes financial sense. Just remember the point of life insurance is not to act as an investment, it is intended to cover final expenses and ensure your family has the financial resources needed until they can provide for themselves.

Riders

Insurance policies state specific dollar limits on certain items they cover. In order to raise those limits or perhaps cover specific scenarios, you may be able to purchase insurance **riders**. Think of these as "add-ons" to your insurance policy. Riders are popular in life insurance, but are also available in homeowners and auto insurance as well.

Bottom Line: Consider Life Insurance when you start a family and it is recommended to stick with term life insurance and be intentional about investing the rest.

Health Insurance

Health Insurance on its own will be the second largest expense you will have, housing being the biggest. Health care delivery is always being debated and until the debates get settled you need to take it seriously. The easiest way to get access is through an employer. Typically this requires full time status. The employer will cover the cost of your health insurance plan or subsidize it (help pay for it). The downside is if you are accustomed to not paying a health insurance premium every month because it is covered at work and you lose your job, then the financial burden compounds. You are now looking for a job *and* also paying an expensive premium.

There are different types of Health Insurance, here is a very basic primer of some of the more traditional options.

HMO

An HMO is the base level of health care. **HMO** stands for "Health Maintenance Organization." The idea is to maintain health. Typically, this is not an ideal plan if you are constantly sick or injured. The expense structure of the plan is typically lower monthly premiums (but still expensive), lower out-of-pocket costs, and may or may not include a deductible. The structure is in-network only (except for medical emergencies or if care isn't available in the network). What this means is there is a specific list of doctors you may see, and only these doctors. If you want to see a specialist, like a dermatologist, then a referral from a primary care doctor may be required. The goal is for the health insurance to reduce costs and they do this by regulating what you can and can't do and who you can and can't see. In general, if you are healthy this works ok.

PPO

PPO stands for "Preferred Provider Organization." This type of insurance typically means higher monthly premiums, higher out-of-pocket costs, including deductibles. However, there is much more flexibility to see providers both in and out of the insurance network. You want to see a dermatologist? Go for it. No gatekeeper or seeing the primary care physician first. There may be a doctor you would like to see, but they do not accept HMOs, so you would need to "upgrade" your plan to a PPO in order to see that particular doctor. This takes some planning as you cannot just "upgrade" plans on the spot.

ACA or Obamacare

Obamacare, also known as the **Affordable Care Act**, or ACA is a law enacted to ensure that all Americans have access to affordable health insurance. It is not a health plan, but aids access to healthcare. There were some laws changed like allowing children up to age 26 to stay on their parents' plan. The ACA also addresses pre-existing medical conditions. In the past if you had an issue like diabetes, you could be turned down for insurance or your cost for coverage would be too much. There was also the creation of health exchanges or marketplaces where people can try to get the best price for health care.

Similar to life insurance, if you sign up for an HMO by yourself, you would need to complete some health questions. There isn't a health exam required. And if you get health insurance through an employer, you are not required to fill out a questionnaire.

Very similar to how P&C insurance works, you pay a premium every month. It includes a base amount of services or set costs. For instance, you pay your premium and then if you visit your primary care physician for a check-up or a physical, you would pay a "**copay**" which is a small amount of money to see your doctor. It could be $10 or $20; it all depends on your plan. It is usually very inexpensive. The same goes for prescriptions. Let's say your medicine costs $200, your insurance will cover most of it, but you would need to pay a small amount (again copay) for the medicine. Side note: Medications in some cases are becoming competitive in pricing, it is worth checking out sites helping find discounts.

If you have a need beyond the basics, such as surgery, then you would be paying a deductible. This amount would depend on the type of insurance you bought and the amount of your premium. A simplified explanation would be if your knee surgery costs $35,000 and your deductible is $5,000 then once you pay $5,000, the insurance company covers the other $30,000.

With an employee sponsored plan, there are a couple other healthcare benefits options you might be offered:

Flex-Spending Account or FSA

The money you put into your FSA is similar in style to a traditional IRA. The amount you contribute to this account is pre-tax. If you make $50,000 and put $1500 into an FSA, then you are taxed on $48,500. The difference of course is this money is for health-related expenses only and not an investment account. This requires a little bit of planning because the money you put in has an expiration date (the year). If you don't use it, you lose it! So, if you have some predictable health related expenses, this is a good option. If you are generally healthy or you cannot specifically lay out what you will spend on your health, then it isn't necessary.

Health Spending Account or HSA

These accounts are similar to FSA, but allow you to roll over any amount you don't use. The money can also be invested! If you withdraw funds for non-qualified expenses before you turn 65, you'll owe income taxes on the money plus a 20% penalty. The issue here is the HSA requires a High-Deductible Health Plan. This can be really expensive, but HSAs (if you qualify) are the best of the two accounts.

Bottom Line: Do not mess with healthcare. Budget this early and NEVER risk it or go without insurance. The downside far outweighs any extra money you save by not paying premiums.

RETIREMENT

(401k, 403b, IRA, Roth, Traditional, etc.)

If you are a connoisseur of memes you may know the "hide the pain Harold" meme. It is a stock photo of an older man who appears to be hiding his pain behind a forced smile. I would like to suggest the pain Harold is hiding from is the fact he did not plan ahead for his retirement. Some of you may be thinking, "retirement? I am just trying to pass a math class! Why should I worry about retiring?" Remember at the outset we talked about the magic of compound interest and how time is a key ingredient in compounding. The earlier you start, the better chance you have to avoid the same "pain" as Harold. Plus, these accounts have tax advantages.

But don't just imagine old people retiring. There is a niche group of people who sock away as much as they can so they can retire at like age 30! (look up F.I.R.E or *financially independent retire early* investors).

Here is another example of why starting NOW matters. Assume you have two options.

Option 1: You start with $500 and at 18 you start to contribute $200 a month into a retirement account. We will assume a 9% return annually. Then at age of 32 you stop, let it run another 30 years with no more contributions, and you retire at 62.

Option 2: You wait until you are 32. You finally have a stable job so you start with $500 but to "catch up" you contribute double the amount ($400 a month). You do this for 30 years assuming 9% return annually until you hit age 62.

Here are the results:

With option 1, you will have earned $64,116.92 at 32. If you let it run without any more contributions then at age 62, you will have: **$850,682.68**

With option 2: At age 62, after 30 years of contributions you will end up with **$660,910.02**

Notice that even by contributing more money for a longer period, the delay in contributing results in almost $200,000 less than getting started earlier!

If you also noticed in the example, there was an assumption of a 9% return. Where did the 9% come from? Certainly not from bank interest! These retirement accounts are similar to brokerage accounts in that you can decide where and how to invest your money. You could invest in one company (not recommended because of our discussion on diversification) or you could invest in all sorts of funds, bonds or even gold.

Contributing money is the first step. Then you need to have a plan of what type of account and what to invest in.

First, the different account types:

IRA. IRA stands for **Individual Retirement Account**. This is an account which comes with tax advantages because you are saving for your retirement. Whereas a regular brokerage account does not come with tax advantages (income and capital gains).

If you choose to open an IRA you have two options: **Traditional** or a **Roth**.

Traditional IRA means the money you put into the account gets a tax deduction up front or for that year. If you earned $25,000 in income for the year and contributed $1000 to your traditional IRA, then your taxable income now becomes $24,000 ($25,000 - $1,000 contributed).

The money you contribute grows in the IRA and then when you take money out at retirement, you will get taxed at your income tax rate.

Roth is the other option. A Roth IRA is named after Senator Roth who proposed this option to increase a little more tax revenue for the government up front because of the traditional IRA tax deduction delaying tax revenue. The trade-off is the government taxes the money now, but it will allow that money to grow in an account. When you take a distribution (take money out) there will be no income tax on the backend.

Again, if you earned $25,000 and contributed $1,000 into a ROTH, your taxable amount for the year is still $25,000. But, the $1,000 grows in value and when you take money out at retirement age, you do not pay income tax.

There is a limit to how much you can contribute to an IRA (to limit your tax advantage) and as of publishing the limit is $6,000 a year.

Retirement accounts can also be tapped for funds early, but it comes with a cost. If you withdraw money from these accounts early, you are on the hook for a 10% early withdrawal penalty plus you are taxed at income tax rates. This can be a huge hit to your retirement. Avoid, if you can.

Roth accounts do have some great advantages. There are options to take money out of this account with no penalties. You can look these up, but here are some things to consider. You may withdraw contributions you made to your Roth IRA anytime, without penalty or tax. Note this is a contribution. So if you contributed $200 to a Roth (which has been taxed already) and it grows to $500, you can take $200 out without penalty. Once you go beyond that threshold, you are on the hook for penalties and tax. There are a few reasons you may be able to take money out early on your growth or earnings. Look this up for yourself, but one which is interesting is you may take up to $10,000 out to pay a down payment on a first-time home purchase.

Bottom Line: Have you set up an IRA? If not, definitely worth looking into to set up your future and perhaps reduce your tax burden.

401k

Blake: Whoaaa whats a 401K?
Ders: Basically its a retirement plan so you can...
Blake: Oh, nevermind. I totally thought it was a laser[10]

Another retirement option that could be available to you is a **401k**. A 401k simply refers to the section on employer sponsored retirement plans in the tax code, but don't worry about the code.

Employer sponsored retirement plans means there are jobs or employers offering a benefit to workers to help them put money away for retirement. These are not mandatory, hence "work benefit" or "perk," but most do. 401k plans can vary from place to place but here are some things to know.

401k benefits are typically given to workers who are full-time or

---

[10] Workaholics

work enough hours per week. If you work part-time, the chances are you do not have access to this benefit.

Assuming you have access to the benefit, a 401k works very much like an IRA. You elect how much of your paycheck goes into this retirement account and select a type (Roth or Traditional). Just like a traditional IRA you reduce your tax burden based on how much you contribute. (Again, if your gross income is $50,000 and you contribute $2000 to a **traditional** 401k, your taxable income becomes $48,000).

Some things you should know and look for if you are offered a 401k through work:

First, check the **vesting provisions**. Vesting is a word to describe how long you have to work with the company before you can start to contribute. If vesting is "immediate" then you can contribute as early as your first paycheck. Some companies may require 3 months or 6 months or even a year. If your company offers a plan but has a longer vesting period, do not sit on the sidelines. Remember you are letting time slip away, which could be working for you. Contribute to your own IRA and contribute a portion of earnings there. To consider how much to contribute, the flippant answer is: as much as you can afford!

Second, the other piece of information you want to find out about the company 401k plan is to ask if there is **matching**. Matching means your employer will match up to a certain amount of what you contribute. Matching differs from employer to employer, but to give an example an employer may match "dollar for dollar, up to 5%." This means your employer will match what you contribute up to 5% of your income. If you contributed $300 from your first paycheck, your employer will also kick in $300 into your 401k. $600 went into your 401k that month! Nice! Assuming your contribution isn't above 5% of your paycheck it will be matched, dollar for dollar.

As mentioned, there are several different ways employers offer matching so be sure to ask about it. While you could contribute more than 5% it won't be matched after 5% and it is advised not to go beyond or contribute more than the matching amount. The reason is simple, 401k plans can be fee heavy. If you have more you can put away, put it into your IRA or other asset instead.

Here is a basic understanding of how they work. Your employer sets up a 401k plan with a company specializing in these plans. When you enroll, you are typically given a limited amount of options on what you can invest the money in. Unlike your own IRA where you can invest in most anything, these plans are reliant on Mutual Funds. If you remember, Mutual Funds are good for diversification, but can be expensive to operate and may eat away at your gains. (Revisit the section on Mutual Funds).

The standard option is to put you into a **Target Date Fund**. This was discussed earlier, but as a reminder this is a fund with the objective of investing based on your age. If you are younger and you select a Target Date fund, the fund will be more aggressive. If you are on the older side and get a Target Date Fund, it tends to be more conservative with the goal of helping you preserve income as you approach retirement.

These are convenient as you don't have to think and you can just shovel money every paycheck and watch it grow over time. As always, check their fees and expenses. The convenience may not be worth it.

Depending on your job and employer they may offer plans with other strange numbers like **403b** and **457**. These are essentially the same as a 401k. The reason they are labeled differently is because if a non-profit organization offers a plan it is called a 403b and if you work for state or local government agencies it is a 457b. We can distinguish these plans further, but this is sufficient for an introduction as they operate very similarly to 401k's. Finally, a **SEP IRA** is for self-employed people. As an "employer" of themselves, they can contribute to a retirement account more like a 401k despite it having "IRA" in the name. If you are self-employed be sure to look into these.

Bottom Line: Just remember in the craziness of a new job be sure to participate in your company 401k plan, especially if they match.

HOUSING & TRANSPORTATION

Car buying is becoming more simplified with apps and websites so we won't walk through the entire process, but here are just a couple things to keep in mind. The most financially responsible way to acquire a car is to buy a used car in cash. The reason is you pay for what the car is worth and avoid the extra you pay to finance it (loan plus interest, etc.).

With brand new cars, the second you drive off the lot, the car **depreciates** (loses value) substantially. Here is why. A consumer would always choose a new car over a used car if the price is close. Therefore, the market price of a used car even with 1 mile on the odometer drops in price in order to compete. Even though you lose value on the car immediately, you are still paying interest on that lost value from day 1. This is explained further in the gap insurance section to follow.

There may be reasons why this used car paid in cash option may not work for you, so we'll look at a few options for a new car.

Your payment options for a new car are to **lease** or **finance**. Lease is a fancy word for rent. The benefits of leasing are you get to drive a new car every 3 years or so. Since the car is technically not yours, the dealer is responsible for all the service and oil changes on it.

The downside is the interest rate is typically higher than financing (buying). Also, because you are technically renting the vehicle, you may have to pay extra for anything beyond normal "wear and tear" when you return the car. There are also strict mileage restrictions set annually. If you go over your mileage, which can range from 10,000 to 12,000 miles a year, you may have to pay per mile (10 - 30 cents on average) over that amount when you turn in the car. If you choose a lease, just make sure you know all the fees and penalties. Sometimes you can negotiate mileage restrictions and other details prior to signing.

Financing is where you take out a loan, pay off the loan over a period of time and you own the car outright. The technical term, **lien** (pronounced lean) means you have an obligation to pay a loan or debt. Your car is technically owned by the **lienholder** (or the bank that issues you the loan) until you pay it off. Until you remove the lien, the lienholder can rightfully seize the car. This would only arise if you failed to make payments.

Financially speaking and all things being equal, buying is usually the better deal over the life of the car. You pay less for it, and get more equity out of it than a lease.

Typically, a car is financed over 5 years or 60 months.

Once at the dealership, one method to get you to commit to buying a car is to ask, "what would you like to pay per month?" This seems amazing at first. The dealer will work with me on my monthly payment? Yes, BUT the payment length just gets extended to make your monthly payment look nice. You may have agreed to pay for the car for 7 years instead of 5 years. And while your monthly payments are less, you pay more for the car in the long run. Always keep your eye on the purchase price. This is what you want to negotiate, not the payments per month.

The purchase price begins from the **MSRP** (manufacturer suggested retail price), which is really designed to anchor you.

Meaning, it makes you feel like you are getting a deal if you pay less than MSRP. But it was anchored high to begin with leaving plenty of room for negotiation (the exception of course are brands like Tesla in which you buy direct and not from a dealer). The MSRP is not the price of the car and it is certainly not what the dealer paid for it.

At the dealership you may also have the option to trade-in your current vehicle for cash or to reduce the purchase price of your new car. Just know, this will always be at the lower end of the car value. It is convenient, but you will lose out on some equity.

When buying a new car, it is recommended to do a web search of your car make, model, trim and year with the word "forum" or "message board." It'll take a little work but you want to find a site where people are posting on message boards what they paid for the same or similar car to yours. Take your time, and do your research. If you are in a rush and are impulsive you just won't get the best deal. This is an emotional purchase. Stick to your numbers, your budget, and take the time to research. Don't be afraid to walk and pick back up later.

For both leases and purchasing, you do pay taxes and fees. Be sure to visit your state's motor vehicles website to calculate your actual taxes, license, and fees on the car you are getting. The dealer calculates it for you, but it is always good to know exactly what you are expecting to pay just in case there is a discrepancy. If you do not pay these taxes and fees up front when you purchase, then this amount gets added to your payment and gets financed as well (wrapped up into the loan).

To summarize, cars are not assets but liabilities (the exception being classic or rare cars). Be smart. It is understandable if cars are important to you, but don't get trapped.

Gap Insurance

When you finish up your time with the car salesperson and get handed over to the "finance person" you will get offered **gap insurance** among a lot of other add-ons. Here is the idea behind this insurance. Imagine saving up for a brand-new car and the day arrives when you finally get it. The car was a 2021 $35,000 DeLorian (it doesn't exist, but really should). You pull out of the dealer and immediately get t-boned by another driver. You are livid but you have insurance so you call up your insurance agent and after filing a claim you get a check for $31,000. You call up your agent because there must have been a mistake since you just paid $35,000. The agent says, "no, you get actual cash value and a 2021 used car with 1 mile is $31,000." You say, "wait, no I just bought it. It's brand new." The agent responds, "no, the second you buy the car and drive it off the lot, it becomes a used car." In this case, you lost $4,000. This is **depreciation**.

But the good news is there is a type of insurance you can purchase which covers the "gap" or difference. This insurance is not too expensive and is usually offered by the dealer. It isn't required, so it is up to you.

Real Estate & Mortgages

Cars may be a big expense, but housing will be your biggest living expense. The general rule of thumb is you do not want to spend more than 30% of your gross income on housing. There are parts of the country where this is really difficult to do. But like a car, you have the option to rent or buy (mortgage) a home.

Renting. When looking for rental properties, the price is listed as a monthly payment. As you compare with your budget, one thing to keep in mind is the cost to move in is substantially higher than you think. When you find a place to rent and it's quoted as $1,000 a month, the cost to move in will most likely include a credit check cost. The person or company renting the property needs to check your credit and this can cost around $80 or more. This cost is passed on to you.

If you are approved, then you will be asked to pay a **security deposit**. This money is "security" for the person renting you the place and held for the duration of your stay. This is to be used if you damage property beyond normal use. When you move out and the place is in good shape, you will get your security deposit returned back to you. Another request from renters is for you to pay the **first and last month's rent**. This is to make sure they do not lose out on money if you decide to bail out early. All in all, you might be paying $2,500 to $3,500 just to move into a $1,000/month property. This payment is also paid upfront. Unlike a restaurant where you pay at the end of your meal, with renting you pay for the upcoming month.

Keep in mind with renting there are usually utilities you will need to pay. **Utilities** are services like electricity, natural gas, water, trash, internet, phone, etc. Some rental properties include water and trash and some do not. Be sure to ask. You will need to price any utilities and bills into your monthly budget.

Real Estate. Buying a home is a more involved process not just in terms of financing, but even the phrase "the joys of homeownership" facetiously refers to the high maintenance and upkeep required. Therefore, it is worth stating that buying a home is not always the best option even though you build equity.

It all depends on your situation.

Without getting into all the details, here are the basics:

Buying a home is like any other loan for the most part but it does carry its own cute name, **mortgage**. This word has its roots meaning *death pledge*, i.e.: the loan dies when you pay it off. Like a typical loan, you apply for a loan to finance this large purchase. The amount you can borrow is based on a lot of factors such as your credit, how much you make in income, and how much of a down payment you can make.

Mortgages have many nuances which are beyond the scope of this introduction. Financing, for instance, can come in a variety of options. One is a **fixed rate**. This means the interest rate you pay stays the same throughout the life of the loan. Another is an **ARM**, or **adjustable rate mortgage**. This is typically offered as a lower rate to start then adjusts later. This is designed for those who do not plan to stay in the same home for that long.

When buying a home there are other expenses to be aware of. Down payments mean you are required to pay upfront a certain percentage of the cost of the home. This is intended to make sure you are serious. The down payment could be as low as 5% but 20% is desirable.

PMI stands for private mortgage insurance and is required by the lender or bank if you are making a down payment of usually less than 20%. This is insurance you pay monthly so the lender can recoup losses if you stop making mortgage payments. Usually, PMI is satisfied with a bigger down payment but not always. This can be .5 – 2% of the loan or somewhere between $30-$75 for every $100,000 borrowed.

Property taxes are another expense to be aware of. They are assessed and paid semi-annually. These payments are quite large and are typically used to pay for local services, roads and education (schools). Every county and city are different, but in a very general sense that is how property taxes work. The U.S. average is about $2,400, but again the range for you could be much higher.

Finally, there are real estate agent commission fees which can be around 5% of the cost of the house. Both sides one way or another end up kicking into this.

When you find a house that you want to buy you submit an **L.O.I.** or **letter of intent** expressing your intent to buy the home. Agents and brokers can help you with this. The intent also includes contingencies. In other words, you may have the intent to buy the home, but only if there are no plumbing issues or all inspections get passed, or shrubs get removed, or "cottage cheese" gets scraped off you're the ceiling etc. You may also state a contingency on your end like, "we intend to buy if we get a loan," or "if our job relocating us here gets finalized."

Since this is not an eBay auction and the seller can sell to whomever they wish, they may choose to sell to someone with less contingencies even if they offer less money. It all depends on their needs.

A seller accepts a bid, papers are signed and so the "waiting period" while contingencies are being met is called **escrow**. There is also what is called an escrow service where the buyer places the money with this third-party escrow company meant to act as the objective party in the transaction. Mainly, they hold the money and distribute it to the seller if and when all the contingencies are met and the buyer gets the **title** (a document that states you legally own something) to the house. And of course, the buyer's financials and credit are sufficient.

A house may "fall out of escrow" when a contingency or a loan fails. The house then goes back "on the market."

That was the 30,000 foot view of home buying/selling.

Once you have been approved and start paying off your mortgage, an aspect worth noting is equity and lines of credit. As you pay off your mortgage, the process of **amortization** occurs. This fancy word simply means the process of paying off debt. As you begin to do so, you start building equity (which if you recall means ownership). You are acquiring more and more outright ownership of your house from the bank.

When you do that, it means you can leverage that equity if you need to. Let's say you want to upgrade the kitchen in your home. One of the ways you can finance this is by getting a **HELOC** or home equity line of credit. On a simplistic level, if you have paid $100,000 of your $600,000 house you could leverage that $100,000 ownership for a **line of credit**. Similar to a credit card, you are given a limit of up to $100,000. When you draw from it, you pay interest on the amount borrowed until you pay it back. If you don't, it could result in the house being foreclosed (or being taken back), so be careful. Some people will also take out what is called a **second mortgage**, which is the same concept. The difference is instead of a line of credit, you get more of a lump sum of cash, or in this case a loan for $100,000.

There are so many other layers such as "points" and "origination fees," but this is sufficient for a basic introduction. Feel free to talk with real estate agents or mortgage brokers about the entire process.

Finally, since this expense is so high, there is wisdom in figuring out how you can reduce this burden through other investment rental properties or by renting out sections of the house to offset your costs. Imagine what an extra 30% of your income could do in the market or some other asset! Feel free to investigate further and look into concepts like "house hacking." Until then, enjoy Zillow Gone Wild.

I keep hearing about "2008," what happened?

There are tons of books and documentaries dedicated solely to this topic, so our purpose is to not to give a full analysis and history but rather give a quick overview of part of what happened. Recall that earlier we talked about Treasuries. For investors and even nations around the world, they are looking for safe, steady investments to preserve their income or reserves. Treasuries have long been considered one of the safest. Plus, they pump out some interest as well. Long story short, the amount of interest these treasuries were paying started trending on the lower end and our monetary policy decided we would keep it that way for the foreseeable future. This was a buzzkill for global investors. But there was another investment which was deemed almost as safe and pumped out even better interest. These were and are called **mortgage backed securities**. Think of it as a mutual fund filled with mortgages. So, you have thousands of mortgages with monthly interest payments getting kicked into this fund every month. Owning a slice would be a nice investment. Imagine getting a piece of the action on thousands of mortgage payments. Needless to say, these got really popular.

To back up a little, remember that when you get approved for a mortgage, there is a lender or bank which bought the house for you and you are paying them (typically) for 15-30 years until it is paid off. This is not the greatest investment for them because they get small amounts of interest and have to wait a long time to get their money back. In large quantities it's good, but still a long wait to get the maximum return. But the other option is that they can sell *your* mortgage to a larger, institutional bank. Nothing really changes on your end, but your mortgage payment now goes to the institutional bank. The big institutional bank buys tons of these mortgages from smaller banks and lenders and packages them up into the mortgage backed securities which we likened to a mutual fund.

They can then sell slices of this fund to investors and make money there too. Because there are debt obligations in these slices (mortgage loans), investors want to know they are safe. So, a bond rating agency gives a grade. These grades range from AAA down to C. The better graded funds (AAA, AA, etc.) are deemed safer and do not yield as much interest. The B's and C's yield much more interest but they are riskier. High risk, high reward.

What was happening leading to 2008 was that these mortgage backed securities got really popular. So popular in fact that demand couldn't meet supply. There was pressure from the institutional banks for lenders and small banks to get more mortgages. In order to do so, the rules had to be loosened. Up to this point, since this was such a big loan you needed to have good credit, and actual proof of income. The lender would double check and make sure you could actually afford the house you wanted. But when there was a demand to write more mortgages, the rules got really loose. So loose, you only had to state your income. There was no double checking. You literally could get a mortgage for an $800,000 house, and they would ask how much do you make? You could say "oh, 1.2 million," and they would approve it! Even if in reality you were unemployed or worked at Arby's.

More and more mortgages were being written. More and more loans were being given out to people who had no business affording these homes. This created a **bubble**. This means there was a highly inflated number of houses being mortgaged. And like bubbles do, they pop. More and more people defaulted on their homes. Meaning they couldn't make their payments. Tons and tons of money was lent out and never paid back. Lots of money was lost in these investments and multitudes of people lost their homes.

The movie The Big Short (based on a book) is about some people who saw this happening. They also noticed there was another debt security being sold called a **CDO** or **collateralized debt obligation**. This was a way to sell those lower graded and risky mortgage slices, because they weren't selling. The investor appetite globally was for safe and highly graded mortgage backed securities. What they did with the poorly graded and/or unsold mortgages was to create a new product. The CDO would contain these undesirable mortgages, but then also add in other loans as well, like auto loans or small business loans. This brand new CDO had all sorts of random debt obligations in them. There would be a stream of payments coming into the fund and investors could buy shares. The thing is, even though the fund was filled with "toxic" and bad mortgages, the ratings agencies saw this as a new thing and slapped a good grade on them. Their reasoning was "strength in numbers...not all the loans will go bad." Even if a mortgage fails, it'll be fine because there are more debts and mortgages in the fund to make up for it.

To thicken the plot, insurance companies offered an insurance product called a **Credit Default Swap**. Which very simply means, you pay for a kind of "insurance" on the product (on the CDO) and if it defaults or fails (payments stop), then the insurance will "swap out" the bad CDO and pay you what you are owed.

The geniuses in the Big Short saw this collapse coming, so they bought a bunch of these Credit Default Swaps for about 2% of the total assets as a premium cost to hedge against default. And this is why they benefited and made so much money because they in essence had "insurance" (not technically, but like insurance) and got paid out on a bunch of defaulted CDOs. This is why in the film it is likened to being able to buy fire insurance on a burning building. The difference is I cannot buy fire insurance on your home, only mine. But a CDS could be purchased without owning the assets.

As the bubble burst and people couldn't make payments on their mortgages, banks and insurance companies had to request a bail out from the government to prevent them from going completely bankrupt. Depending on who you talk to, the country was within hours of total economic collapse. The economic recovery took a long time which is why you hear "2008" spoken of as the Great Recession.

Lesson: if something seems too good to be true and there is a lot of hype, there may be a bubble about to burst. Who knows, student loans may be next!

CONCLUSION

Congrats on completing your beginners' journey through the world of personal finance. You have graduated from calves and cubs and are ready to engage the world of bulls and bears. This is only the beginning! Don't be afraid to dig deeper and learn more and ask more questions. You are responsible for your own education. Knowledge is great but it only becomes wisdom when you apply it. If you desire to be wise with your money and finances, you need to act. To help you plan, please complete the Personal Action Plan.

The purpose of this Personal Action Plan is to have one place to work through your personal finance goals. At the very least, going through this will put things on your radar and hopefully get you to think twice before making financial decisions. Many times in this document you will be asked to not just state your goals but come up with a system. A system is a way to accomplish the goal. Let's say you want to save more money each month. You put a system in place that says every time a $5 dollar bill comes into my hands, it goes into a savings account. Good idea or not, that is a system. Another system might be, if I cannot pay off the purchase right away then it isn't for me. I will keep saving.

Let's begin!

Savings/Emergency Fund: Part 1 - Do you have at least $1,000 in emergency funds? If not, what is your plan to build that reserve starting TODAY? WHERE will you deposit this money?

Plan/Goal:

System:

Preventative Debt Strategy - If you are planning to borrow any money (credit cards, student loans, car loans, etc.) what is your plan to keep it under control? Credit cards are predatory in nature and most people are not disciplined to use them properly, why are you so sure it won't bury you? **What is your system?**

Planned Debts in the next 10 years (credit cards, loans, etc.):

System to stay whole and not get crushed by Credit Cards, other loans, etc.:

Retirement/Investing - Have you started an IRA (individual Retirement Account)? If not, what is your plan to do so within the next month? Will you choose a ROTH or Traditional? Through which provider? How much will you contribute and what specifically will you invest in and WHY? If you are still dependent, have you talked to your family to see if they will match what you put in?

Plan/Goal:

Investment Options (what I plan to invest in; i.e.: specific stocks, ETF's, Index Funds, etc.):

System:

Philanthropy/Charity - For the good of your mental health, financial discipline and the good of others it is recommended to be generous and give at least 10% of your income to a cause or causes. Please specify what causes you plan to give to. It can be a church or a non-profit. It doesn't need to be 10% but even a small amount helps to get started.

My Current Cause(s):

Amount & Frequency:

Is there a way to also be involved beyond giving money?

Time - Because you are not Human Doings and the point of life is to not just to capture and acquire material things and money, how are you budgeting time to remind yourself of what truly matters? When you think about your life, it is the moments that give meaning to it, not the amount of money you had 5 years ago in your bank account. Creating some margin in your schedule to be present and remembering this truth is critical. If you have never done this, pick one day a week and start by unloading your phone and going into nature or for a hike for a 2 hour session.

This isn't a workout, but a chance to recalibrate on presence, gratitude and being.

System to take a break from consuming, working, acquiring:

Rent/Housing - This will be 30 - 35% of your expenses in life and the first part of your income spent. Start to strategize how you can reduce this amount or have it paid for through other rental properties and investments. This is a couple years off, but either start planning on your housing budget or start figuring out a way to start a real estate savings budget. Be specific. It's better to be specific and adjust than be vague and not do anything. Write your plan below. Be sure to include your system. Meaning instead of saying "oh, I plan to save $20 month" what is your system? *How* do you plan to save $20 a month?

Plan/Goal:

System:

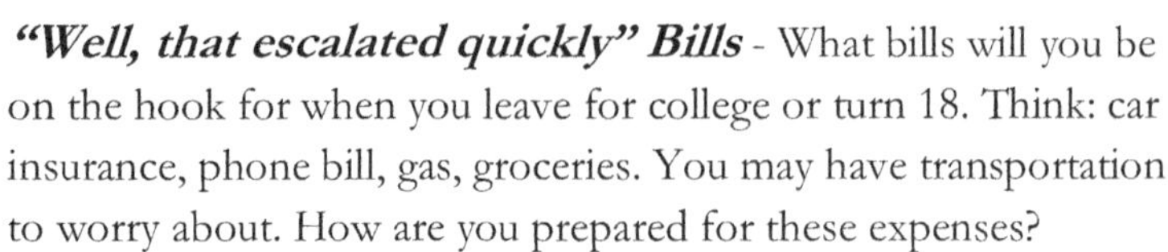

"Well, that escalated quickly" Bills - What bills will you be on the hook for when you leave for college or turn 18. Think: car insurance, phone bill, gas, groceries. You may have transportation to worry about. How are you prepared for these expenses?

Potential Bill/Expense responsibilities (list):

Estimated monthly expense:

Emergency Fund Part 2 - If you are on top of your stuff and no debt, get your emergency fund to last 3-6 months. Imagine a pandemic happens again and you can't work for 3 months straight. Do you have enough to live comfortably for at least 3 months? If so, where is it deposited?

If not, my system is:

401k/403b/SEP IRA - If you start working and the company offers these plans, especially if there is matching…take it! The broker will want to put you in a Target Date Fund. That may be okay or your best option, but LOOK AT THE FEES AND EXPENSES!

Your goal should be 15% of your income (pre-tax) is shoveled into retirement! Anything over the matching amount offered should be in your own account where you have more control over expenses and fees.

My notes/questions

Life Insurance - You can take this more seriously when you get married and start a family. Think about how much you would need to cover your final expenses and give your family plenty of runway to grieve and get back on their feet. Remember the purpose of life insurance is not an investment, consider term before whole life.

My notes/questions

Health Insurance - You are able to stay under your parent/guardian health insurance until age 26. You may want to ask your parents what your premium & deductible are so you have a frame of reference. THIS WILL BE YOUR SECOND LARGEST EXPENSE NEXT TO HOUSING.

My notes/questions

APPENDIX A

I. GRATITUDE

List 10 things you are grateful for

1. ______________________________
   ____
2. ______________________________
   ____
3. ______________________________
   ____
4. ______________________________
   ____
5. ______________________________
   ____
6. ______________________________
   ____
7. ______________________________
   ____
8. ______________________________
   ____
9. ______________________________
   ____
10. ______________________________
    ____

II. GOALS & DREAMS

A. What are the things you want to **HAVE** (material things)?

Short-Term (0-3 years)

____

____

____

Long-Term (5+ years)

____

____

____

B. What are the things you want to **BE** (physically and intellectually)?

Short-Term (0-3 years)

____

____

____

Long-Term (5+ years)

C. What are the things you want to **DO** (start something, go somewhere, etc.)?

Short-Term (0-3 years)

Long-Term (5+ years)

Any other personal notes:

APPENDIX B: *COUNTING* THE COST

NOTE: This section may require a conversation with your parents or guardian. This is your own personal information, so guard it carefully. The objective is knowing your situation and context and what to expect in the future. This helps you with your goals and systems.

I. COUNTING THE COST

Do you have an established monthly budget?

Circle: Yes / No

Do you have a regular savings plan?

Circle: Yes / No

A. **Current Financial Assets in YOUR NAME**

- Checking Account $___________________
- Savings Account $___________________
- CD's $___________________
- Stocks/Mutual Funds $___________________
- Bonds $___________________
- Treasuries or Savings Bonds? $___________________
- IRA (Roth or Traditional) $___________________
- 529 Plan or Coverdell (college fund) $___________________
- Cryptocurrency in USD $___________________
- FOREX in USD $___________________

B. INCOME

i. Any Current Income (student, not parents)

(include allowance, freelancing, side hustles, salary, bonuses, commissions, rental income, interest & dividends, social security, annuity or pension income, and any other income sources)

Income Source	Gross Amount	How often?	Net Take-home amount

ii. Other (Student) Assets (Real estate owned; automobiles, boats, etc.; collectibles, antiques, etc.)

Item/Description	Current Market Value	Cost Basis (your cost to acquire)

iii. Emergency Fund

How many number of months do you have to provide for Emergency Funds? _______ Months

OR: How much do you need monthly in case of an emergency?
$_________________

How much do you currently have saved in a dedicated emergency fund? $_________________

C. PERSONAL MONTHLY EXPENSES

Expenses **YOU** are responsible for. If a parent covers it, find out the amount anyways, write it down and make a note.

Auto & Transportation

Gas $_________________

Car Insurance $_________________

Car Loan / Lease Payment $_________________

UBER or Public Transportation $______________

Service (oil, tires, etc.) $_________________

Other Car expenses $_________________

Education

Tuition $_________________

Books/Supplies $_________________

Food

Dining Out with friends $________________

Lunch at school $________________

Groceries $________________

Coffee Habit $________________

Other Habit(s) $______________

Health / Medical

Insurance Premiums $________________

Prescriptions $________________

Other health/medical $________________

Household

Cleaning Services $________________

Clothing $________________

Gifts $________________

Landscape Service $________________

Personal Care Items $________________

Pet care $________________

Sports & Lessons $________________

Other $________________

Other Monthly Expenses

Subscriptions/Memberships $________________

Tithe/Charity $________________

Gaming & Entertainment $________________

Vices $________________

Other $________________

Add them all up! Total Monthly Expense:

$__________________________

D. LIVING EXPENSES (Ask your parents for these figures, you need to know cost of living)

Mortgage/rent Payment $________________

Homeowners insurance $________________

Other Insurance $________________

TV (cable, Netflix) $________________

Electric $________________

Gas $________________

Internet $________________

Mobile Phones $________________

Trash Collection $________________

Water $__________________

Other Utilities $__________________

Total Monthly Living Expenses:
$_________________________________

E. **OTHER DEBT SERVICE PAYMENTS (total owed, very rare—you personally won't have these yet)**

Credit Cards $__________________

Personal Loans $__________________

Student Loans $__________________

F. **ESTATE?**

Does your family have a Trust?

Circle: Yes / No

If yes, what kind: ______________________

Purpose of Trust: _________________________________

Do you expect to receive any lump sums or inheritance in the near future?

Circle: Yes / No

If yes, do you have a plan?

NOTES AND QUESTIONS

ABOUT THE AUTHOR

Beau Brannan is a Visiting Professor at Pepperdine University. He has taught several personal finance courses to high school and college students. Beau has previously earned his FINRA Series 6 and 63 licenses. He is also involved in the entrepreneurship space and has authored The Entrepreneurship Teacher Playbook. This book was designed as a reference book and gift for students completing the course. His website is brannan.tv and @misterbrannan on Twitter.

For more resources visit: calvesandcubsbook.com

Made in the USA
Las Vegas, NV
22 January 2023

66087067R00104